When YOU Grow UP and get... Single

When YOU Grow UP and get... Single

Surviving & Thriving as a Party of One in a Table for Two-Sized World

When You Grow Up and Get Single
Surviving and Thriving as a Party of One In a Table-for-Two-Sized World

Copyright © 2009 by Stephanie Huffman

Chapter head quotations available on the Internet: http://thinkexist.com.

Cover design and illustrations by
Maureen O'Brien Illustration, www.Mo-Illustration.com.

All rights reserved. No part of this publication may be reproduced, stored in a retrieval system, or transmitted in any form or by any means—electronic, mechanical, photocopying, recording, or otherwise—without the prior written permission of the author. The only exception is brief quotations in printed reviews.

ISBN: 978-0-615-31246-0

Second Edition

*To all the single gals who dream of growing up
and getting married …
may you find your happily ever after.*

Contents

Foreword 9
Preface 11
Greetings & Salutations 13

Part 1: The Sisterhood 15
Chapter 1: When You Grow Up and Get Single 17
Chapter 2: You Are Not Alone 21
Chapter 3: Someday Your Prince Will Come 29
Chapter 4: Cheaper by The Dozen 37
Chapter 5: You're Just Too Picky 45

Part 2: Personal Matters 53
Chapter 6: Happy Holidays 55
Chapter 7: When Your Pet is Your Kid 65
Chapter 8: Travel Well, Travel Right 73
Chapter 9: Home Sweet Home 79

Part 3: When Life Happens 87
Chapter 10: What Doesn't Kill You 89
Chapter 11: A Divine Holiday 101
Chapter 12: Lay Offs, Life Changes, and Other Scary Stories 107

Part 4: Goals and Dreams 115
Chapter 13: Out of the Darkness and Into the Light 117
Chapter 14: Charting Your Course to Success 125
Chapter 15: How Do You Eat An Elephant? (One bite at a time.) 135
Chapter 16: Going for the Gold 145

Part 5: Living Large 151
Chapter 17: Golden Girls 153
Chapter 18: Single Is a Subculture 159
Chapter 19: The No Sex in the City Club 165
Chapter 20: Starting Your Own Chix Chat Club 177
Chapter 21: Random Confessions of Single Females 185
Chapter 22: The Upside of Living Single 191

Until We Meet Again 197
Acknowledgments 199
Source Notes 201
For Further Reading 203
About the Author 205

Foreword

I'VE commiserated with cohort Elizabeth Taylor about our mutual theme of "Don't date, always marry," and I'm embarrassed to say I've been "Mrs." enough times to make-up for every "single" gal about to read this revealing book.

Stephanie is a close friend, major wit, and—without exception—an asset to anyone's speed-dial. Her candid take on singleness and all that comes with it provides a handbook for navigating the seas of "singles" labels and self-questioning. Singleness is not a disease or a devastating disaster, but rather a state that one finds herself whether by choice or circumstance. Personally, I'd rather be "alone and not lonely" as opposed to "together alone", but that may be easy for me to say since I've felt the reality of both conditions all too often.

Within these beautifully crafted pages, Stephanie shares her own war-stories as well as her relationships with friends, that will inspire honest dialogue and openness as she draws readers into the fold of a safe and a healthy overview of their desires. This book's woven together with tender persuasion and profound caring; it offers a positive plan for achieving happiness.

In *When You Grow Up and Get...Single,* author Stephanie Huffman aptly points out that knowing she's not the only one who shares fanciful dreams, crazy thoughts, fears, expectations, and disappointments sheds valuable insight and light on a girl's journey to fulfillment. Understanding that we don't have to swim the solo waters alone is a vital part of charting a course to personal success

If you're not married, *When You Grow Up and Get...Single,* is a must read! And if you want to better understand a single friend's world, this book is a must! After all, what are friends for if not to laugh and cry together and to understand, lift-up, and love each other, unconditionally?

Thanks for sharing your heart, Steph. You rock!

xo Jen

Preface

YOU know what it's like. You enter the restaurant and the hostess looks up and inquires, "How many?" You shyly look away, maybe clear your throat, and decide to confidently reply, "One, please. Just one."

And we girls usually add something like, "Is that OK? You can seat me anywhere. Really. I have some work to do. You know, reading. Things …" Your voice trails off as you pad behind the hostess who leads you to a twenty-four inch table squished against a post or balustrade while trying to house two tiny chairs. It looks to be a tight fit, but you'll make it work.

You try to organize your accoutrements and prepare to settle in. It's going to be a long night, and you might as well enjoy it and the coming cuisine. You've done this before. And you'll do it again. And again, and again, and again …

Greetings & Salutations

"Tea for two, and two for tea, Me for you, and you for me."
—Irving Ceasar

I own approximately four full sets of china and stoneware. My mom jokes that I need more dishes. When my cousin and her family of five came to visit me one summer, we could have eaten all week on my collections and never washed dishes—once. We could have just set them in the backyard and kept going through the cabinets. I am pleased to report that we ran the dishwasher. A lot!

I just love china and silver. I love to entertain, and I love to eat. But I've found that people do find it a bit odd that Stephanie, a single girl, has the ability (and the desire) to feed a party of twelve at the drop of a hat and produce a full, silver tea and coffee service post meal. If that is not enough, I have a complete collection of homemaking books, cookbooks, napkin and towel folding books, etiquette books, and parenting books that take up precious space on my shelves. I have never given one of them away, and I don't plan to. None has ever made it to Goodwill: they probably won't. I keep thinking that one day I will need them all. Why? Because deep down I hold that underlying, undying, relentless internal hope that "it" too can happen to me—the big "M".

I'm talkin' about marriage.

I've come to believe that the desire to be married is universal for most women. I find that the majority of girls I meet, speak with, or observe think about marriage at some point if not most of their lives. They just pretty much plan to grow up, get married, and have a family. That's normal. And it's okay.

Years ago I carried a piece of paper listing the names I would choose from when it came time for my first child. (Which I *knew* would be a boy.) I knew, too, that one day (post wedding of course), I would host holiday gatherings, prepare scrumptious and creative meals, and plan educational and memorable family vacations. With this future in mind, I saved linens from family members and purchased them while on trips to the various countries I visited. I collected all types of culinary tools, articles, and recipes. I even devoured any etiquette book I could get my hands on as a sort of preparation hobby. Forever filing away educational guides that would teach a child history or how to read, I made constant notes on how to be a good wife and mother. Without a doubt, I knew that when I grew up I would be the best mom and homemaker ever.

It never happened. Well, at least, not yet.

Stacks of books, china, silver utensils, and a stuffed hope chest later, I am still, yes, single; but that's not to say I've given up on my dreams. In the meantime, while I wait for my happily ever after, I have decided to find and align myself with other single girls like me. I am committing myself to helping other solo sisters out there find each other; I'm making a concerted effort to personally improve and, in turn, encourage other single girls along the way. That's why I've included an entire chapter (How to Start Your Own Chix Chat Club) to help you find like kinds.

But for now, it will be just you and me. Our own little circle of sorts that we'll create as we journey these pages together. I've included at the end of each chapter some Chix Chat questions that I hope will connect with you and help you discover what's really going on in that heart and mind of yours. At the back of this book, I've included my web address: please e-mail me with your responses and comments. I'd love to hear from you!

I guess you could say that I have personally made a concerted effort to enjoy the life I've been given. Now, I'd like to share it with you! It truly is possible. This single phase of our lives can be a unique and exciting adventure. It's just that it's up to us. We can do it. As fashion designer Tim Gunn likes to say, "Make it work, people. Make it work." 'Nuff said.

So, here we go …

Part 1

The Sisterhood

Chapter 1

When You Grow Up and Get Single

I don't know when it actually happened. But at some point in my life, I woke up to realize that I had not grown up and gotten married; instead, I'd actually grown up and gotten —single!

As I started to survey the solo waters of my life, wondering why I was so alone, I felt relieved to discover other like souls floating past in their own ships of singleness. I duly reached out, grabbed, and threw those people into my own boat. (After all, it's always safer to sail with a buddy.)

It was as if I were in search of like minds to which I could say: "Please. I need to know I am not a mutation or accident or something that went awry in the evolutional relationship chain." I needed to know that other women, out there somewhere, woke up one morning to find, like me, that they too had simply grown up and gotten single.

If you picked up this book, chances are pretty good you've finally hit that point. Think about it. Whether you have not yet married, have recently divorced, or find yourself an unsuspecting widow, unless you beat the odds, it will happen. You, too, will one day find that you have grown up and gotten single. However, lest you fear this book will leave you feeling that life without a man leads only to shipwreck, don't bail out on me just yet. Marriage is great; but you, my solo sister, and I are about to embark on an excursion. We'll discover opportunities to build great memories along with a wealth of encouraging news specifically geared for those that are currently sans spouse.

I am proof that what I claim about singleness is true. And take it from me: Life as a single really isn't so bad. In fact, it's actually pretty good of late. If I can survive this phase of life, so can you. You are going to be just fine. Life as a single *can* be an exciting adventure.

As you might imagine, writing about singleness did not rank among the "Top 10" on my list of to-dos. I just assumed that at some point in my little life I would join the myriad of women who live in proverbial, yellow houses with white picket fences. You know, those with two kids, two cars, and a dog in the yard? I spent most of my forty-something years wanting to be married. Happily married, I might add. But did I grow up and get married? Not yet. Am I happy? You know, I'd have to admit—I am.

My original intent in writing this book was to share nuggets of wit and wisdom solely with my not-yet-married circle of friends. To encourage them. To promote discussion. And to just plain give them an opportunity to let off the steam that builds when some guy at work gives them a hard time because no husband will retaliate or when that nosey individual asks for the hundredth time, "So, are you dating anyone special?"

It soon became clear that there was a heartfelt message I wanted to share with *every* single girl. If you find yourself asking, "Does anyone else out there feel this way? Am I the only one that's been through this? Do other single gals think like me?" this book's for you.

Good news, my friend: You are not alone. Every emotion you have felt, and might feel now, has been felt before, and will be felt again by one of your single sisters. Together, we travel a unique path, a largely uncharted journey. And at times the road, though a little intimidating, can be pretty hilarious.

You may not be in the mood to embrace the single lifestyle, yet. I understand that. But I've found it easier and more enjoyable to experience life's adventures with others. That's why I invite you into my life and mind and into the lives of a few amazing single gals who sail the singleness waters with me. In the pages ahead, I will attempt to address your questions, acknowledge your fears, and assure you that, no matter where you stand at this time in your life, you will not only survive this season of singleness, you will come to thrive in it.

The information we will ponder together is derived from hours of phone conversations between other non-married gals and me. We've talked at all times of the day and night and have held multitudinous heart-to-heart chats at various eateries and coffee shops around town and across the world. Some of the ideas you'll discover come from the wisdom of friends. Others reveal how I make the solo lifestyle work for me.

Through the coming paragraphs, I will show you that other single ladies out there refuse to feel like incomplete jigsaw puzzles with gaping holes that scream, "The last piece is missing!" Instead, many women—girls just like you and me—are learning to successfully navigate their way as parties of one in a table-for-two-sized world.

Before we get started, put this book down for a second. Go make your favorite cup of tea or coffee. Then curl up on that sofa, cozy chair, or that "luxurious" airline seat (preferably in the upright and seated position). Join me for some much-needed girl time. We'll call it Chix Chat.

Chix Chat:

1. What is your current attitude toward singleness?
2. What frustrates you the most about living on your own?
3. List three perks specific to living as an unattached female.

CHAPTER 2

You Are Not Alone

"I'm going someplace I've never been before ... Alone."
— *Unknown*

ONE day, it occurred to me that I'm probably more qualified to expound on the singleness topic than I ever realized. While I didn't think about it until I started the whole book ordeal, my life has been greatly influenced by single ladies since my girlhood. In fact, I may have been prepped to write this little tome since I was but a pup.

DIVORCED

I suppose my story really begins with my grandma's. My grandmother was a knock out. As a young woman, she married a very nice man who looked like Ronald Reagan. He was athletic, a couple of years older than she, and played the trumpet. Together, they ministered to the down-and-out population of 1930's Los Angeles.

Unfortunately, as the young man grew older, he developed a bit of a problem with alcohol. Soon, my grandmother found herself a divorcée with two children—an uncommon dilemma in the 1940's. For my grandmother, there was definitely no plan "B" in place, nothing to guide her through the situation. Over the next month, she climbed over numerous obstacles in the new single world. For instance, in order to keep and stay in her apartment, she had to appear before a board of men who ran her building. She was judged and tried, forced to petition for permission to work off the nine months back rent her husband owed.

To make ends meet, she worked in a little fast food drive-in across from the junior college, collected bottles for cash, and served her girls chipped beef on toast. My grandmother not only survived her trying times, but she ended up owning her own Escrow company, which had three different offices in Southern California. Not bad for a single mom with no mentor or role model—especially since in those days women rarely grew up and got single by divorce.

WIDOWED

In the not-so-distant past, widowhood was the primary contributor to singleness. My mom can testify to this. My mother was also quite striking. She was married to a super guy and had a little girl. (That's me.) One day, when she was thirty-three, she learned that her thirty-six-year-old husband had cancer and only three months to live. Four months later, he was gone. He left behind a very small life insurance policy, but no real savings. Just an eight-year-old daughter. My mother had a high school education, but that was it. It never occurred to her that she would grow up and get single by widowhood. My grandmother's company was a blessing in that it provided my mother employment during part of that turbulent time.

These two women were my world. My family unit, so to speak. We lived and breathed each other for twenty years of my life. All of life's joys, tears, and adventures we faced together. I wouldn't trade those times with those two amazing single ladies for anything in the world!

My grandmother and mother supported every move I made. They were always there. At every performance and in the front row. With bells on. (Well, not really, but you get the picture.) They were determined to make sure I had the opportunities in life that they missed. They wanted me to succeed and enjoy the things they did not have during their youth. As the child of two generations of single moms, I not only attended a private, four-year University, but I traveled extensively and lived in Los Angeles for a semester to study acting professionally for college credit. I am more than grateful for Grandma's and Mom's loving support: I am humbled and moved to tears when I think about it.

NOT-YET-MARRIED

Ironically, whether I realized it or not, I grew up learning to be single. I was in training from the get go. All I really knew and understood was the world of singles. My grandmother had been single all of my life, and I was raised by a single mother. Interestingly, they never expected me to stay single. It never crossed their minds. Or mine.

I lived in a house with parents for only eight years of my life. I don't remember much from that period. I do, however, remember my parents' arguments. They upset me. But you really aren't attuned to relationships at that age. You think Mom and Dad will always be there. Maybe, that's why I didn't take notes.

Growing up, I learned what it meant to mow the lawn, to manage the finances, to do the check book, to deal with the car when it broke down, to prune the fruit trees, to hang the Christmas lights on the house, and to shop for, drag in, and put up our own tree. Mom and I didn't have a man around to do those things for us. Responsibility fell on me early.

Sometimes, I look around and say, "Wow. How did get here?" I have no kids. I never married. I, like my grandmother and my mother, find that I too grew up and got single.

Some ask, "So why didn't you marry when you had the chance?" I came close. Twice. But I just couldn't take the leap. I knew deep down I had something to accomplish in life that just didn't include any of the men interested in walking down the aisle with me at those times. I do not boast about that. It wasn't what I wanted or planned; I just stayed true to my heart. I couldn't lie to a man who loved me, pretending that the gnawing "There's something down the road waiting for me … calling me" feeling wasn't there. The last thing I wanted was a miserable marriage that ended in a divorce. And so, I keep waiting for the one man with whom I can wake up for the rest of my life. In the meantime, I'm making the most of each moment.

Over the years some folks may have assumed that my situation never posed a proper male/female, family environment. "You were not ready for, or groomed to be capable of, marriage," they might say, as if that might explain why I have no husband. "You had no training." Fine. I can live with that. But I see a lot of marriages that consist of two people who did not evolve from Beaver Cleaver households or environments that make it work. A perfect early family life is not a prerequisite for a happy marriage.

I work hard to make sure that I do not focus on my singleness as something to endure. I truly do strive to embrace its positives. And I intentionally look for them. For instance, I do not have an "ex-wife" factor in my life or in-laws living in my basement who slowly drive me to insanity. Furthermore, I am not living with a man who makes me secretly wonder if he will care for me should I go senile. I don't wonder where my husband is and with whom he spends time when he's not with me.

For today, it's just me and the dog; and we're doing pretty well.

My grandmother always said, "There are worse things than being single." Singleness is far preferable to rushing down the aisle into an unhappy, lopsided marriage. While I would love to find Mr. Right and get married, I know that marriage is work. Hard work. That's why it's something I want to do with a partner who wants to work at doing life together just as much as I do.

WHAT ARE THE ODDS?

When I first began researching for this book, I was amazed at how singleness—especially for those who have never been married—is still viewed as a potential disease, illness, or even a curse. Odd indeed when you realize that approximately ninety-two million people in America (as of this writing) are single.[1] Many places around the world share similarly high numbers: their stats are rising, too. It's stranger still when you look at the number of unattached celebrities plastered on our magazine covers and television screens every day, who—when they do marry—usually return to singleness again within a few short months or years.

Remember the television show *Sex and the City*? That drama was not a hit because all of the women were married. It was successful because they were singles trying to *get* married! Those hip, city girls lived out a new trend. And the same phenomenon played out on sit-coms *Friends* and *Seinfeld*. In fact, if you take a good look, you'll notice that very few hits from the last two decades featured *Leave It to Beaver* or *Father Knows Best* families. Newer, hotter shows reflect the single culture that resonates with people. Take a look at these statistics.

> "There are worse things than being single."

America hit a new record in 2006. That year the total number of single adult men and women made up forty-two percent of the national population for adults eighteen years and older.[2] That meant that, for every one hundred adults you met that year, forty-two were single! Not only that, sixty percent of those singles had never-been-married. And fifty-four percent of those singles you met were women.[3] What that said to me was this: the traditional family featuring father, mother, and two kids no longer represents "every" American home. According to the U.S. Census Bureau, there are now eighty-six single men for every one hundred single women. Unmarried Americans are the fastest growing demographic group.[4]

I was surprised to also learn that over thirty million Americans live alone.[5] They, too, comprise a significant percentage of all households. Amazingly, forty-four percent of all U.S. homes are being maintained by single individuals.[6] That's almost one half!

Why such large singles numbers? Why the growing number of men and women choosing to live individually? The experts have been tracking the trend. In 2000 thirty-one percent of men and nearly forty percent of women were married.[7] By 2006 only a little over twenty-three percent of men and thirty-one percent of women in their twenties were married.[8] Some blame the rising divorce rates. But one major factor behind that shift that caught my attention is that the percentage of those marrying in their twenties continues to decline.[9]

> *According to the U.S. Census Bureau, there are now eighty-six single men for every one hundred single women. Unmarried Americans are the fastest growing demographic group.*

Jean Twenge, author of *Generation Me: Why Today's Young Americans Are More Confident, Assertive, Entitled—and More Miserable—Than Ever Before* concludes that today's young adults feel happiness only comes from being self-sufficient.[10] For some reason, young Americans view emotional relationships as weakness. Our culture not only accepts it now promotes and accommodates the single lifestyle and tends to look down on the individual who isn't committed to advancing themselves.

But I don't believe that Twenge's findings prove that singles are to be simply dubbed as "self-centered". Singles, according to the statistics, are anything but merely self absorbed or, rather, selfish people. In fact, in an article dated March 10, 2008, the Association of Fund Raising Professionals reported that unmarried women contribute more to charity.[12] The giving of those single females surpassed twenty-three billion dollars.[13] I would imagine charities in the twenty first century will be found focusing on us savvy, single girls!

> *Trivia: In 2004, the number of unmarried girls over the age of 30 in Saudi Arabia was more than 1.5 million.*[11]

GET THEE TO A NUNNERY. OR, MAYBE NOT.

If you're anything like me, you may sometimes feel like the quintessential fifth wheel. But if the statistics are any revelation, you and I are actually becoming part of an increasingly well-noted majority. We are becoming the norm: an assertive, giving norm at that.

We didn't plan the trend, and I'm not saying I'm glad it's the case. The truth, however, is that the world of coupledom, on which civilizations were built and for which so many of us long, is rapidly dwindling in size and popularity. Singleness is on the rise: you and I are hardly alone.

My ninety-four-year-old grandfather and I chatted about this trend toward singleness shortly before he passed away. He blamed lack of opportunity: "There were more chances to mingle back in my day," he said. And he's right. If you think about it, there were get-togethers, state fairs, picnics, parades, and more. In his day, things like church socials were expected and accepted norms and must-attend events. Their culture was built on a type of fellowship and social-gathering mentality. He felt more social interaction led to more marriage and "proved" it by reminding me that he met my grandmother at a barn dance where they served hot apple cider.

Gramps may have been onto something. Our generation is isolated and alone most of the time. Even our daily interactions are done not face-to-face but over the Internet.

DOUBLE, DOUBLE TOIL AND TROUBLE

Blame the divorce rate, or the fact that people are marrying later in life, or even the unfortunate fact that some men just flat dispose of their current spouses for better, sleeker, or richer models. Regardless of the why, a whole lot of singleness is going on.

Perhaps your family and friends relay the impression that, since you're single, you are only half a person who is waiting for and should be desperately seeking your missing part. Perhaps, they leave you wondering if you're incapable of properly developing and maintaining a relationship. Maybe, they even make you feel guilty about your single status—as if you brought the situation on yourself.

So, here's the deal. If you and I continue to feel incomplete in this new world of singledom, how on earth are we, as perfectly functional, intelligent beings supposed to exist–let alone thrive? If you feel like a jigsaw puzzle with a gaping hole where that final, missing piece should be, hear me say, "You are going to be O.K. And, you're going to make it!" My wish is to come along side of you and encourage you not to freeze in paralysis, bemoan your lifestyle of freedom, and question your past decisions. Stop mourning those ice cream and DVD infused dateless weekends my friend, and join me in discovering that:

1. You are not alone.
2. There is a world out there that awaits your brains and beauty, and
3. Believe and understand that you can successfully navigate the solo waters that surround you.

It is my hope that my friends and I will be of comfort when you one day wake up to find that you, too, have grown up and gotten single. You will not only survive this current journey, you will thrive once you realize that you are a perfectly normal member of this not so new–but very trendy–people group.

Chix Chat:

1. Consider the demographic of your current circle of friends. How many are single? Divorced? Widowed?
2. How many single men are in your circle?
3. Consider the people in your life who say, "You're too picky." Who makes you feel singleness is a curse? Why is it important that you not take their words or attitudes to heart?
4. Do you spend more time with people who are single or married?
5. What benefit might you gain or what opportunities might you lose as a result of spending most of your time with this group?

CHAPTER 3

Someday Your Prince Will Come

"I had the serendipity of modeling during a temporary interlude between Twiggy and Kate Moss, when it was actually okay for women to look as if we ate and enjoyed life."
- Cybil Shepherd

NO particular reason or pattern leads to singleness. No magic formula brings Prince Charming to one girl's door and a hunting party of Mr. Wrongs to another's. Some people like to chalk it up to bad karma. Poor timing. The bottom line is this: things happen. Life happens. Even for those who do get engaged or married, happiness isn't necessarily a guaranteed part of the contractual agreement.

Consider this true story. A thirty-seven-year-old girl finally met Mr. Wonderful. They dated, got engaged, and began planning their wedding. One day while he was at the gym, Mr. Wonderful heard a loud pop. Heading home to do a bit of research, he went online to discover that he had experienced an aneurism. He walked himself immediately to the nearest hospital where, upon arrival, he went into a coma and died.

The woman he left behind was horrified. Why, oh why, did such a tragedy happen to her? She had waited so long. Questions flooded her heart and mind, but no real answers surfaced.

Some people try to explain away all tragedies by ascribing them to God's will, but I think that could lead people to feel as if God is unjust and unloving. I think we're better off not blaming Him when unfortunate things occur; instead, accepting that things just happen. Trying to figure out why bad things take place or why we remain single is beyond our finite minds. That's why, in this chapter,

I'd like to give you permission to stop asking "what if?" and to quit playing the blame game. Obviously, the woman in the story did nothing wrong. And there was nothing odd about her. She was merely a victim of circumstances that twisted her journey down a shocking new path. Singleness is not something we can understand, predict, avoid, or explain. Further, I'm not sure it's a great idea to overanalyze it.

IF ONLY I WERE THINNER

All of the single women to whom I will introduce you throughout this book are attractive, smart, talented, and fun. They love life. Their pursuits and passions don't fit a formula explaining why they remained single while their high school and college friends went on to marry and have children. These girls don't claim to have the answers or to have uncovered the reasons: they are simply committed to helping each other avoid playing the "Why oh, why?" game.

I have girlfriends who are married—happily married—who are not size twos and gorgeous. As a matter of fact, one friend looks like a Mid-west farm girl. Big and strong. Rarely, if ever, wears make-up. She can fix her own water heater and most anything else that breaks down. No frills to this one. She's as real as they come. But you won't find her on the cover of *Cosmo*. And she'll be the first to tell you she's fine with that.

When I look at the beautiful, successful über women who headline in the news and in Hollywood, I'm reminded that physical attractiveness and sculpted bodies don't guarantee a traditional happily ever after. Many of the celebrities who grace our magazine covers are anything but married. Though successful, talented, and absolutely amazing, the majority of them are single.

No amount of starving yourself and counting calories will assure you happiness—that's just what fashion and fitness marketers want you to believe. Just ask Elizabeth Taylor: a designer filled closet will not secure a long-term marriage. Most of Hollywood is single. Don't believe for a second that you are not married because of your weight or your clothes. If that were the case, the sexy, attractive single celebrities of our world would all have long been married by now.

No matter the path that led you to grow up and get single, you are not a freak of nature. Nothing about you marks you as a woman who will not find happiness or who will not attract a spouse. *You* have the abilities and the potential to be a valuable, exciting character on the stage of life. And I am right here in the front row cheering for you!

Earlier, I encouraged you to find and spend time with like-minded friends. If you are divorced, it's important to find women friends who share the experience. If you are widowed, search out other widows—especially those closer to your age. If you are a single mom, look for gals who understand the responsibilities and the struggles that come with your unique set of challenges. And if you have not-yet married, find those women in your life who are still waiting. That's exactly what I did, and I've never regretted it.

When I hit the fortieth year milestone, I began to feel I was the only one who'd managed to stay unattached. Then one day, it dawned on me that, in fact, that was not the case. I remember sitting down with pen and paper listing women I either knew or had met who were in the same boat as me. Soon I turned that list into a group of friends who became a Coffee Klatch of Five. They became my personal support system, and I love them dearly to this day. I hope you'll gather a group of loving friends around you as well.

So here they are. A few of the girls in my circle. These talented, attractive girls often hear, "You're not married!?" (Translation: what's wrong with you?) These gals would love to be married. But in the meantime, they have committed to making the most of their lives. They are encouragements to me, and I am proud of them. My hope is that their stories will encourage you along your path, reminding you that – though many us sail boats of singleness – we can learn to sail them successfully into new and exciting seas.

The Starving Artist

Like me, **Sadie** is a member of the Screen Actors Guild. While this sounds impressive—especially when coupled with her PhD—she isn't exactly rolling in cash. (Only two percent of the union's acting membership makes over five thousand dollars per year from this profession.[1])

Sadie and I have both done the Hollywood thing, so we share a bit of what comes with that in common. When I talk with her about certain celebrities whom we both have met or come to know through the years, she says, "Oh, yes, I worked them," or "I sang with them." (That's often followed by a line like this: "I knew her when she was getting ready to marry husband number two.")

Sadie is a doll. Cute. Red hair. Vibrant personality. She's had a successful music business for years. Sadie is over fifty-five and has never married, but she has never stopped believing that her Mr. Right is out there.

The Belle

Chloe is an adorable size four who could easily model. I joined her on a trip that took us to Sydney, Australia. The men we encountered there (who weren't gay) looked at her pretty, Southern self. They didn't even notice me! (Come to think of it, she even got kissed by a koala, while I got kicked by a kangaroo.)

Chloe has worked with some very well-known authors, traveled internationally, and done video interviews. She's great under pressure and with people—politely internalizing things that bother her rather than speaking her mind. (Whatever comes into my mind, by the way, usually exits my mouth.)

Chloe is hip and just plain cool. But I can assure you that she simply isn't interested in putting her life on hold until Rhett Butler comes along. She wouldn't mind, though, if he suddenly called her out of the blue and asked for a date this weekend! She is over 40 has not not-yet-married.

The Explorer

Gracie spent two years in Russia teaching English. She has floated down the Amazon River. And she did a couple of weeks in India. Gracie's an adorable blonde who exercises religiously. She's five foot three. Tan. Sporty.

Gracie's family currently puts a lot of pressure on her to marry and have children. She has been involved with online dating services to try and move things along. She has had plenty of dates. The guys love her. But as of this writing, nothing has quite clicked. Gracie is always bubbly and incredibly positive. She could scale Mt. Rushmore if she wanted to. I love her zest for life and can-do spirit. She too is over 40 and is still on the look-out for her man.

The Ministering Angel

Noel is the tall, blonde daughter of a model and a flying ace. Raised in the military world, Noel is very patriotic. She even spent a short time aboard the *U.S.S. Ronald Reagan* as an instructor. The students loved her as she was a very good listener and enjoys encouraging others.

One time, while returning home from helping a friend, Noel saw a car in front of her suddenly flip multiple times. She stopped to help, though the victim—a college student heading to campus—didn't make it. In Noel fashion, she contacted the funeral home (which was states away) and ended up connecting with the girl's mother. She assured the grieving parent that her daughter was not alone when she died.

When I think of Noel, I think of someone who embraces life as it comes. No holds barred. She will be the first to encourage those of us in her circle of friends to do the same. Also having passed the fortieth milestone, she would love to find her own special guy.

The Earth Girl

Elle is one of seven children. Raised Irish Catholic, she has a very "groovy" spin on life that can only come from a zany familial environment. If the world ended tomorrow, Elle would be there to clean up, offer counsel, and then rise like a phoenix from the ashes.

She eats completely organic foods and is always on a detox of some sort. She's incredibly healthy and doesn't need a drop of makeup. Ever the artist, she is a hand illustrator by trade and runs her own business. (To see her work, check out the beautiful job she did on my book cover!) Elle has managed not only to buy a new house but owns a few rental properties. When I grow up, I'd like to be her. She's a role model to me.

Elle will be the first to tell you that approaching fifty as one who has not-yet-married is tough. But hope springs eternal. She patiently waits.

The like souls of these very fab friends who come alongside me in my journey of singleness are such a blessing. These gals just plain rock! However, regardless of their talents, successes, and attractiveness, these women will be the first to tell you that they are normal, flawed humans—not so different from any of those girls who do have husbands. My purpose in introducing them is to show that there is no explainable reason why these amazing women are still not married. For them, waiting has not been easy. Yet, they are choosing to make the most of their current lives. We, as a group, are committed to helping each other chart these unknown waters of singleness. I sincerely hope that you too will surround yourself with friends who share a similar life path and that you will gather together as we do.

You know, some days I go to my refrigerator, see the names of my dear friends held there by a magnet, and find such solace in looking at their names.

"I am not alone," I say aloud when I see them, "I am *not* alone."

SINGLE ISLAND

It's interesting that women in the early twentieth century fought for freedom from men. The freedom to vote. To wear short skirts. To gain careers and own property. Nowadays, we spend most of our time and money trying to attract a man who will come to our rescue, love us, and take care of us forever and ever, amen.

The life of the single gal can be likened to one of those vote-someone-off reality television shows. Only it's like most of us are actually hoping for a chance to get booted out of this lonely hearts club. I refer to it as Single Island. Wouldn't it be great if once a week one of our single friends was actually voted off our island and into happily married life?

When my girlfriends and I get together for our chat time, we laugh about this. The inner circle schemes over lattes about how to find the best way to get voted off the island. Obviously, we have not yet unearthed the secret since we are all still single.

I find it ironic that many married women think we singles have it made. They envy all of that "free time" we have, and some even think Single Island sounds romantic. I *think* I understand. While wives and mothers are knee deep in dishes, evening bath time, and homework, it must seem that a girl like me is lounging in a bubble bath with a chardonnay and classical music. Maybe, they even picture me out in my high-heeled shoes having martinis with the single set. (I actually met a guy from Israel who really thought that's what we do!) Of course the truth is that we single gals have our hands full.

A friend and I mused about this subject while enjoying cheeseburgers one evening.

"You have got to address in your book all of that 'free time' people think we supposedly have," she said, "It's exhausting!"

I knew she was right. So I brainstormed a list of things we single girls handle that might result in our feeling a bit weary now and then. Here are just a few of the items on my list that came to mind:

Clean the house. Pay the bills. Clean out the car. Keep the car maintained. Remember to get gas. Do the laundry. Water the plants. Take that item in for repair. Try to fix that other thing myself. Remember to get stamps. Go grocery shopping. Cook then clean up. Replace light bulbs and air filters. Do the yard work. Take the dog to the vet. Walk the dog. Remember to buy the Heart Guard™ and flea meds. Brush the dog. Keep up on insurance changes and needs. Make medical appointments and then actually go. Call to have the gutters cleaned. Load the dishwasher then remember to unload it. Return and send personal e-mails. Don't forget to allow social and online time with friends. Go to worship service and related activities. Allow phone time with friends and family. Shop for and purchase that birthday gift. Don't forget to go to the gym. Help serve dinner at the Rescue Mission. Get bids for repairs on the house. Make that hair appointment. Catch up on my reading. Take out the garbage. Again. And then work. And work some more…

Here's to all the free time we single gals share.

Just how and when's a single girl supposed to date and get voted off the island? Now, if you'll excuse me, I'm off to clean the refrigerator.

BIRDS OF A FEATHER

In the last chapter, I asked you to consider your circle of friends. If the women you spend time with are married and you are not, you will eventually find that you just cannot relate on many matters. Be honest. Do your married friends really want to hear about how you dropped everything in order to head out for dinner and a movie with one of your best girl pals while they were at home bathing the kids, cleaning up after dinner, and throwing in another load of laundry? Or, better yet, does your married friend need to know how you had such a terrible day at work that you put aside all housework or the to-dos on your list just soak in a hot tub before retiring early? Of course not.

> *Your circle needs to include girls on a similar life path.*

Now, I'm not suggesting that you ditch your friends with spouses; but you might need to adjust how much time you spend with people with whom you can't really relate. Your intimate friends, those with whom you pour out your heart, need to include girls on the same wave length or at the least on a similar life path as yours.

SO, WHAT'S A GIRL TO DO?

We live in an age when producers and directors can constantly select yet another group of women who'll happily agree to parade in front of a carefully selected he-man for a reality-styled love-a-muck show. Personally, I find it sad how many women in America alone are willing to expose themselves (and their hearts) on national television in search of a mate.

Remember, practically one third of America is single! When you do the math, there's probably a lot of *desperate* women among them. But you and I don't have to be counted among them. You and I *can* develop positive self-images, if we so choose, and are willing to commit to doing just that. It's time we rally together and encourage one another to do our best at every turn.

Chix Chat:

1. How many of your friends have not-yet-married? Of those, how many are over thirty-five? Divorced or widowed?
2. Consider your friends. How many of them are a size four or smaller? Look like cover models? Have it all together? What, if any bearing, do any of those factors have on their relationship status?
3. Respond to the statement, "Looks, size, and clothes do not promise a loving marriage."
4. Describe your closest single friend. Write her a note listing things about her that you admire. Don't forget to mail it. You'll make her day!
5. When did realize you had grown up and gotten single? Journal your story.

Chapter 4

Cheaper by The Dozen

"Marriage was a goal. A family, for me as a young girl, was my image of what I hoped for. It was part of the big picture."
—Demi Moore

IN the last chapter, I mentioned the value of building friendships with women of like backgrounds and experiences. While every single girl has her own unique story—and certainly a divorcee's biography differs from a widow's—most who grew up and got single can agree on one thing: the world at large seems to take exception to the idea of a female remaining unattached. Unfortunately, this attitude leads to a host of unpleasant encounters and emotionally charged questions with which we've got to wrestle.

I'll never forget the day my Atlanta cab driver slammed on the brakes as he pulled into the Ritz Carlton's driveway. "We are here to marry and have children," he announced in a pronounced Indian clip. "That is our purpose."

By some twist of fate, I got stuck with the most talkative cabbie in Georgia. From the moment he discovered I was in town for the writer's convention, he peppered me with questions and launched into parental advice mode. As we zigged and zagged our way through the city streets, he kept yanking my wandering mind back to my upcoming book and its content. Suddenly, I found myself laying out the theme.

"That is a good book," he announced. "But I am still surprised you aren't married. What is your criteria for marrying?"

Clearly he'd determined that I was not living up to my potential.

To be honest, I was stumped for a moment. I truly didn't have my "talking points" down on this one. In fact, I didn't have a running list of requirements for potential mates at all.

Years ago I had such a list. But now—as I grow much more aware that what I expect and look for at this juncture may not be what will come my way—I've stopped obsessing about a potential mate's body type or age. Nowadays, it's about how a future husband might treat me. Would he share my beliefs? Would we share the same worldview? Could he handle me? Challenge me? Confront me? Would we make a good team? Would he truly love me? *Me?*

"What you must remember," said the driver as he pulled to a stop, "is that we are here to marry and produce children. That is our purpose in life!"

To be honest, I was stunned. I practically fell out of the cab, my mind swirling. I walked away from the car without even paying, and the observant doorman was kind enough to catch me and remedy my error. It was then that I felt hurt and frantically started second guessing myself. Thoughts spun and my emotions rose as I walked into the elevator and watched its door close. Was the cabbie right? Had I failed in the life purpose assigned every human? Had I truly been too picky with my love choices? Was I missing out on life because I didn't just marry when the opportunities arose?

Heading into the reception hall, I prayed frantically and silently: *God in heaven, if I have erred, You can solve it. You can make it right. You are the God who parted the Red Sea and healed the blind. Nothing is too hard for you. And You forgive. So please, forgive me if I messed up big on this one. Come through for me. Show me if I made a mistake in choosing this path. You fix things. Fix this for me.*

Within a few hours, the sting of that taxi cab encounter wore off and I began to realize—perhaps in part by divine intervention—that the course of my life is no mistake. It's okay that I don't have a husband. It's perfectly all right that I don't bounce a baby on each hip or have a teenager begging for my car keys. Of course, I know all this. But the cabbie's words haunted me.

PARTY FOR –TWELVE?

If you haven't seen the movie, *Cheaper By the Dozen*, you should. It travels through the journey of a family with a very full house. And if you don't remember this old saying, "With six you get egg-roll," which became the title of a movie as well—check it out! *My Big Fat Greek Wedding*, the older film *Yours, Mine, and Ours*, and even television reruns of *The Waltons* can brighten a long day. Something about big families makes us girls smile. We love stories about bustling kids with mishaps and victories, harried moms, and ultra cool dads. The excitement, the drama, and the angst those families face seem to inexplicably draw us. For some reason, many girls grow up planning for or dreaming of a very big, bustling brood to call their own.

I'll never forget the words that exited my single friend's mouth when I casually asked her about the craziest purchase she made while on her dream trip through Italy and France.

"I bought a gorgeous table cloth with matching linen napkins for twelve!" she exclaimed. "If anything, I can give it to my children someday."

I just smiled. Only moments before she told me that she didn't see herself ever marrying.

When the words about posterity slipped from the mouth of this unmarried, childless beauty, I didn't say a thing. I didn't want to lose the moment. She was—at least for a bit—continuing to believe in the dream. I nodded and smiled and encouraged her to talk, knowing her purchase pointed to what seems an inherent part of us as women. We don't plan to grow up and get single. Some of us just do.

ALWAYS A BRIDESMAID ...

From the time we are wee girls, we put towels on our heads that doubled as bridal veils and marched down our own make-believe aisles. At a very early age, we act out and plan our weddings. No one teaches us to do it. Instead, the play seems to arise naturally from some place deep down in the very fiber of our beings.

One afternoon in late high school, a classmate and I sat in her kitchen and discussed her bridesmaid dresses. She had selected the pattern, the material, the shoes. Everything was in place. Everything, that is, except a groom. In fact, she wasn't even dating. Nevertheless, she had the entire plan mapped.

I never got that far in my imagination. I never planned for or played out my wedding ceremony in my head. I did, though, plan to marry. And I guess I thought it would happen sometime in my late twenties.

Some girls plan life in detail. They've got an education plan. A career plan. A get married by such-and-such date plan. They've determined the number of children they'll birth, how far apart they'll be spaced, and what their names should be. Other girls, like me, just know there's a whole lot of life to live and assume that everything—career, husband, offspring—will happen in good time. The world offers amazing opportunities, and I remember feeling the excitement and the potential that lay before me as I set out to college. But while I didn't have a plan in place regarding my future relationships, I am sure of one thing: I have had that "when I grow-up-and-get-married" mentality for as long as I can remember.

TWENTY-SEVEN DRESSES

Perhaps you caught the movie *Twenty-Seven Dresses*? In it a darling, hard-working, blonde finds that she is always in weddings. Unfortunately, they're never her own.

A while back, a friend invited me to her fortieth birthday celebration. We guests were treated to a PowerPoint™ presentation of my friend's life to date, a slide-show autobiography of sorts. When we got to the "bridesmaid" photos, a voice from the rear of the room asked, "Are we going to see photos of *all* of them?"

At first, no one quite knew how to respond; but soon my table of single gals doubled over in laughter. I literally had tears running down my face. Why? Because we could all relate! Our closets are stuffed with dresses from wedding parties. None of them from our own.

I have a pretty healthy collection of bridesmaid dresses. I can already see you nodding your head and saying, "So do I!" Mine either hang listlessly in my closet or are stuffed in my hope chest. While I should sell those dresses taking up precious space in my closet, I just can't. I'm a sentimental sap.

Over the years, I've sung at and/or played the piano for more weddings thatnI can remember. I even once kept a worn, spiral bound notebook with tattered pages showing the names of the couples and the date of each ceremony. Amazingly, and sadly, few of those couples are still married. But that's not what shocks me as I flip through the notebook. Instead, I'm struck with the fact that it never once occurred to me that I would grow up and get single—at least not up to this age. I'm over forty, and the possibility of remaining single this long never even crossed my brain cells in girlhood.

"THAT'S SO AMAZING THAT YOU'RE SINGLE!"

I wouldn't mind a bit if my personal Prince Charming walked into my life and swept me down the aisle, but most days I don't think about that scenario. I take each day, one at a time, with whatever challenges and surprises it brings. To be very honest, I do enjoy my life.

I've got to admit, that at times, I struggle. I don't always like being single. Sometimes, I truly wrestle with the reality of it. Self doubt, anger, depression: they've all kept me company. Generally, I keep such feelings at bay until a scene like this one enters my universe:

I got a phone call a few years back from a gal wanting to order my CDs. (I have done two independent, solo recording projects to date. They take up square footage in my basement, and I sell them out of the trunk of my car or by MP3 download on my website. Please feel free to support the cause.) Anyway, the young caller just could not seem to process that Stephanie, the singer, had really answered the phone. So I finally succumbed to her idea that I was too famous and busy to answer my own line and pretended to be my secretary. We chatted for a few moments as I filled out her order. Then I asked her why "Stephanie's" story and music had meant so much to her. The reply came as a shock.

"Stephanie's so content with being single!"

I gulped.

"I really admire that," she gushed, and for a brief moment I wondered if I had a fellow single girl in need of encouragement on the other end of the phone.

But then came the clincher: "I'm getting married in a few weeks, but …!"

As if someone had flipped a switch in my brain, the girl's voice suddenly became white noise as my thoughts drifted off. Way off. I wanted to hang up the phone. At that moment, I wasn't able to process exactly what I felt, but one thing was for sure: the call was changing the mood of my day, and not for the better. In all honesty, I simply didn't want to hear about how happy she was and how she had managed to land her Mr. Right. Sounds harsh. I know. But true nonetheless. "Sheesh," I thought out loud with my hand covering the receiver. I didn't even know this girl, and she was gleefully expounding my virtues as if she had personally heard me share my heart.

Prior to this encounter, I had not spoken on or addressed singleness in a public format. So I was baffled as to where she was getting her information. In reality, I was honored that she thought so highly of my work and message. But my goodness! There's only so much a post-forty single gal, who isn't even dating at the moment, can take!

Bubbly brides-to-be apparently aren't one of them. At least not on that day.

Here was a girl getting married, reminding me that I wasn't. Not a great way to cap off my current reality of embarking into the next decade. I seriously considered beginning my mid-life crises right then and there.

But I survived.

> **Different is okay.**

One of the greatest challenges we single sisters face is coping with reminders that there's a married club of which we aren't a part. The most important thing for us to remember is that people who are married really do want to see us married too. Happily married. They mean well, and we need to work at remembering that. Especially when the awkward moments come.

Understanding that we as single girls share different world views than our married friends and realizing that we may inadvertently create "languages" of our own within this subculture, we must remember not to write off everyone who says something insensitive regarding our lack of a husband. We can't forget that being different is okay. What matters most is that you and I learn to be okay in that difference.

Chix Chat:

1. When growing up, how many children did you want or plan to have?
2. What names did you choose or consider for your kids? If you do have children, did you give them the names you chose previously, or did you select different ones?
3. Describe the craziest thing you ever purchased for your future life with a husband or family.
4. How many bridesmaid dresses do you own? Describe the ugliest. Your favorite?
5. Why do you think people feel comfortable telling single women they should marry and start families?
6. How might you encourage a single friend who shares an encounter like the one I mentioned in the last paragraphs?
7. Will you participate in or go to a wedding soon? If so, ask a single friend you trust to be on call for you that weekend. Prepare her for the fact that you may be in need of some quick, much-needed phone encouragement during that period of festivities. Go ahead. Call or e-mail her now. Make sure the event is on her radar and schedule. You'll be glad you did.

Chapter 5

You're Just Too Picky

"I'm single because I was born that way."
—Mae West

I have to admit, I am amazed at how some people seem to feel they are fountains of advice for those of us who aren't attached. One of my "favorite" bits of wisdom is, "You're just too picky." This little gem often flies a single girl's way, and I've yet to see the sense in it.

Every time I hear that phrase directed at me or a friend, I nearly bite my tongue in two to avoid saying, "Okay, let me get this straight: The person you're married to now was not the person you were in love with and wanted to spend the rest of your life with. No. Not you. You were simply a responsible adult who one day woke up and said, 'Hmm. It's time for me to marry. This person before me is not that attractive to me. We don't really see eye-to-eye on things. We have very different senses of humor, and we don't have much in common. He or she is, however, a great person; and we're both single. No sense in splitting hairs. I think we should marry.'"

How can any person in his or her right mind possibly think it's a good idea to lay aside discretion and rush down the aisle? I highly doubt anyone has actually done it (Well, maybe in Las Vegas.) I've noticed that the people who most often tell me I am overly-picky are the same ones who literally could not wait to marry their sweethearts—those significant others to whom they are currently bound.

I just don't get it.

Remember that wonderful group of fabulous singles I introduced in chapter three? Well, during one of our fab-five coffee meetings some time after my cab session, Chloe gave us a great piece of advice. We'd been discussing all the bizarre things people say to us singles and the topic naturally turned to the dating thing.

"Never make decisions when you're tired, angry, hungry or PMS-ing," Chloe, the eternal size four, declared.

We all laughed. But, oh, how right we knew she was. How many times have we agreed to a date just to keep ourselves in circulation?

Elle, the artist, broke in with a related story. "There's nothing wrong with being picky. I let my standards down—once. And lived to regret it. I caved to the voices saying, 'You're not out there enough. You work from home. How are you going to meet anyone?' I went out with a guy who was a terrible fit for me. It was the worst thing I could have done. Definitely a bad decision. I won't do that again."

Advice for the single gal does indeed come from a plethora of places. One particular incidence comes to mind for me. During a recent flight, a divorced flight attendant leaned over my seat and asked in all sincerity, "Don't you think it's because your expectations are too high?" *It's* referring to my having not yet married, of course.

I had to wonder. Do people ever ask themselves if their expectations weren't high enough? I guess I may never know.

I'M IN THE MOOD FOR LOVE

During another coffee time with the girls, Gracie announced that her mother recently approached her about the fact that she's still single. Her father had just had a scare in the hospital, and her mom was a bit nervous and worn down after playing nurse. I am sure a lot was on her mind, but I'm not certain anything really excuses her announcement to Gracie: "I need you to fix this." *This* meaning Gracie's lack of a husband.

"I need to know," her Mom continued, "that you will be taken care of when I go. I am offering to pay for any online dating service to help you. Please, Gracie. Fix this now."

Ouch!

"Well, at least she didn't ask if you're a lesbian or something," Chloe added, trying to lighten the mood. "One time my cousin asked me that in all seriousness. It came totally out of the blue."

Let's face it. Our married friends, and sometimes our family members, think we have a problem and they feel obligated to help try and solve it. We are the lonely singles. The misfits. And they just want to see us happy.

In true marriage-minded fashion, a co-worker of mine once asked if he could set me up on a blind date. While in fairness some couples out there love to share their "we met on a blind date" stories, and I am always game to try and see if the stars might align for me, this occasion didn't go so well.

The fateful day was selected, and the directions to my host's home were delivered. I headed out to meet Mr. Possibly Right. Funny. When I got there, this fabulous package of maleness was about six inches shorter than me, had just divorced, and was in the process of building a home that he could not finish because he was actively filing for bankruptcy. As if that wasn't bad enough, he brought his thirteen-year-old son along to stare me down.

I was stunned. Could barely choke down my food. And I wanted to strangle my coworker.

The next day, I did not hold back. When my host asked, "So, what did you think about him?"

I looked my cohort in the eye and, as calmly as I could, replied, "Do you think we are a good match? Is that how you see me? Do you really feel we fit each other?"

What I really wanted to do was scream at the top of my lungs and stomp my feet. But I didn't.

"Why," I calmly asked, "did you set me up with this person?"

He looked at me straight in the eye with the most sincere, dead-pan face and replied...

"You're both single."

Now, there was the wisdom of the ages!

How many times do you want to say to a friend or meddlesome relative, "I am single. Not *desperate*. There is a difference."

You know, sometimes I am tempted to go to the nearest Glamour Shots studio, pay for a sexy photo, and post it in on a billboard near the airport. Below the photo I'd boldly print the question, "Do I *Look* Desperate?"

Sadly, many of the well-meaning people in our lives, try as they might, will simply never understand.

AND THE BEAT GOES ON ...

At one point, I noticed that when one of the girls in our group found herself in a dating situation, the rest of us slipped into a bad habit of questioning and criticizing the actions and words of her new male "prospect." As I mulled over our tendency, it dawned on me that many of us at the table had literally not been on a date in years! I couldn't help but ask myself, *Are we being overly protective, inadvertently encouraging one another to—gasp—be "too picky," or are we just plain jealous?*

Interestingly, a married friend brought something similar to my attention that I honestly hadn't considered prior. Before we single gals ecstatically divulge our latest romantic venture to our friends with spouses, we might want to be a bit more sensitive there as well. After all, they have feelings too.

Think about it. If you have a date this Friday night and the last time your married friend had starry-eyed male attention was twelve years ago, it's only natural that she might feel a little frustrated that she's moved past the exciting dating stage. Be thoughtful and patient when sharing good news about your latest man. Remember, some day the stiletto may be on the other heel.

Finding Mr. Right is truly a process. So, avoid the one or two friends in your pack who are routinely unkind or unsupportive. Be thoughtful towards those who lend you their ears. And, to you lovelies who honestly aren't interested in dating, that's okay, too. Those of us in the solo sisterhood (though difficult for us to process) need to remember that not everyone spells "happily ever after" M-A-R-R-I-A-G-E.

WHERE THE BOYS ARE

I can't close a chapter about the accusation that singles are either too picky or desperate without mentioning two beautiful friends who prove both theories wrong.

One of my very dear friends is actress, model, and author, Jennifer O'Neill. You've likely heard of her. She was the beauty in the timeless film, *Summer of '42*. And Jennifer's modeling career was so impressive that she enjoyed the longest running contract with Cover Girl to date. It's so incredible in fact that her contract sits in the Smithsonian! Jennifer starred in over thirty-one films and has written several books. Hers is quite the life story.

This friend is simply amazing. She's as pretty now as ever. I love going over to her house to find her in customary riding pants (she loves to ride horses), comfy shirt, and sometimes makeup. Mostly, not. We can talk for hours. I never get enough.

Jen is such an icon to me. I love to hear her stories, and I want to drink it all in. I can learn so much from her. She has lived more life than most people will ever see or imagine. Best of all, she's the real deal: I know that when I come to her I'll hear real-world advice from her very real-world experiences.

Everything she has done in her life, Jen has managed to do on a grand scale. She even managed to walk the marriage aisle a record-breaking number of times. Married for the first time at age seventeen, Jennifer found herself "looking for love in all the wrong places."

> "It's not someone else's job to bring me happiness."

Jen's parents shared one of those magical World War II love stories and have been married for sixty-six years. As a young girl, Jennifer went on a mission to find a man who would adore her as her father adored her mom. But though she found fame, fortune, and several husbands, Jennifer could not find the kind of love her parents enjoyed.

Today Jennifer is married to a great guy, and she believes that she's finally found balance. She and her husband are equally yoked since they decided to place God at the center of their union. They're committed to each other and to making it work.

"My relationship with Jesus allows me to lighten up on my husband," she says. "I've learned that the only thing a marriage needs is to have both parties stay." By her own admission, Jen's been single about ten minutes in her life. She knows how to be married, yet, she also has been single. But her lasting advice is the most telling: "It's a wonderful thing when you realize it's not someone else's job to bring you happiness."

My friend Jane has been single about three times. (I think her biography goes like this: single, marriage number one, single, marriage number two, single, marriage number three.) Jane is gorgeous. She is Japanese and is about ten inches over five feet. She is tiny and looks about thirty-five, though I'm sure she tops fifty. Jane will be one of the first to explain that, while sex might get you a man, it won't get you a marriage. She tried it. She knows. And she'll be the first to admit she truly could have stood to be much pickier when seeking a mate.

Jane understands the frustration of being unattached. She's the kind of girl who not only wants to be married, but *has* to be married. She simply refuses to be single. She does *not* like it. At times, she even lived with men. And she is not afraid to say as much. Jane wants a man to help her in the day-to-day grind. A man is her security in this foreign land she now calls home. I can appreciate that.

Jane is now married to a European, whose Russian accent is as thick as her Asian one. It makes me laugh since I can barely understand Jane myself. Trying to communicate in broken English while maintaining a happy marriage takes talent!

I've noticed that when Jane talks to me about her future, she talks in terms of being single. I don't think she plans to divorce. I firmly believe she knows the odds are that she will one day be a widow. I don't even know if she realizes what she says. Somewhere, in the back of her mind, Jane has started planning her future. When she chats about getting "old," no man sits in the picture. Jane talks about moving in with one of her children. Her family is key. She is literally planning for when she grows up and "gets single" all over again.

I find that intriguing.

While Jane prepares for the reality of singleness down the road, I deal with it now. As she mentally prepares for the future ending of her married life, I'm still trying to find one! In the meantime, the off the cuff comments that lead me to question myself will continue to be a part my single world. But Elle's words ring beautiful truth in my ears: "Of course you're too picky!" she confidently stated as she plopped down her five-shot, decaf espresso, "You should be."

She's right, and her words apply to all of us.

Chix Chat:

1. Describe your worst blind date.
2. What does the question "You're too picky" mean? Do you think a person can ever be too picky? Explain.
3. Do you still keep that worn, dog-eared piece of paper with the list of qualities you are looking for in a mate? If so, how has that list changed over time?
4. Who in your circle of friends has been married several times? Have you sat down with that person and talked about her thoughts in regards to marriage for the long term? If not, set up a time to do just that.
5. Who tries to set you up more: your married friends, your single friends, or your family? Why do you think that's the case?

Part 2

Personal Matters

CHAPTER 6

Happy Holidays

"Happiness is having a large, loving, caring, close-knit family in another city."
—George Burns

AH, the holidays. The family table, the chats around the fire, and the conversations I practice in the car as I make the multi-state trek home.

As the miles disappear behind me, I often find myself anticipating the questions and inferences that might await me at my family's various festivities. Aunts and cousins and well-meaning friends will gather round to catch up on the previous months' activities and ventures. In time, they'll start asking questions that may seem perfectly innocent to them, though I wonder if what they're really interested in is the latest scoop on my dating life. (Or, obvious lack thereof.)

"So, uh, Stephanie," a relative might ask, "what exactly have you been doing … er, lately?"

Rather than answer the question, I'm learning to steer the conversation toward updates on their kids or simply default to a story about my dog.

And it's not just the inquiring relatives that want to know. Holidays seem to be a time when online dating service memberships soar. The hunt for a soul-mate hits all-season highs during those special family times. Noel shared with me her humorous twist on this self-matching ritual. She pointed out that, when she's home for the holidays, the divorced guys who haven't already tried to connect with her online, do their best to nail her down for a date while she's in town.

Noel came up with a response to this situation that I find pretty clever.

"The next time I'm home," she claims, "I am going to wear a shirt that reads: I am not your mid-life crises. Please go out and buy that BMW!"

As we embark on this new section, I'd like to touch on some of the personal life decisions and situations unique to us single girls. I also want to discuss family and just how we fit into the extended family unit. If you're like me, most—if not all—of your family members are married with children. This is the case in my family, but I *can* think of one exception. I am pleased to report that I have one very hip cousin who is actually older than me and not-yet-married.

On the whole, the majority of men and women in my family tree are happily attached. And branching out. So, when the "Let's catch up" chats begin when I walk into the kitchen for a piece of pie, this single gal's heart and mind sometimes start racing.

Holidays—including everything from birthdays, to Christmas, to those summer getaways—all are a part of life. But they can pose unique challenges for any single gal.

When I'm home, I like to ask my family members to tell me all about the weekends when they've slipped away with their spouses to some special locale. I am usually kept up-to-date on those outings due to my ninety-one-year-old grandmother's e-mails. (Throughout the year, she sends updates on the entire family.) I hear all about the successes of the grandkids as well as stories about the family vacations. Keeping up with her e-mails proves valuable. I use the information I've learned throughout the year to help me maneuver past the "No men to report in my life right now" moments. Those updates help me steer the conversation away from myself.

I have a most wonderful family. And, too, I am fortunate in that my family is very good to me. When I hear the horror stories from some of my friends—like the one who gets seated at the kids' table since she still doesn't have a spouse—I truly count my lucky stars. My family's not perfect, but I feel blessed to have them, and I could not ask for a better group. I'm not exactly ready to move in with them and set up my senior digs just yet, (for which I am sure they are quite relieved!), but I am truly grateful for them.

Time spent with my extended family—or any family for that matter—can bring about some unexpected emotions. Why? Because it often serves as a reminder that I am ... well ... "different." And being in the midst of those reminders over and over again gets a little personal. The reality is that I am getting older, have not yet married, and am a bit of an anomaly in our ever-growing family tree.

One day I pondered that very topic and just how exactly we single girls fit.

The more I looked at the lineages in the pages of the family tree before me, the more I wondered, *Does my being single qualify me for 'stump-hood?'* I'm not sure how that all plays out in the genealogical world, but you have to admit the words "single" and "family tree" are a bit oxymoronic if you get right down to it.

HEADS UP!

Maybe, it's just something unique to me, but returning home from the holidays can leave me longing for certain opportunities and adventures. Like the ones that the moms and dads in our gathering have experienced with their little families during the year.

If you've found yourself wishing for your own quintessential family outing—the kind we grew up watching on TV or in the movies—you know exactly what I am talking about. As I personally don't have children, the only resemblance to the traditional-style, family vacation takes place when I haul the dog cross-country. I think you'll agree that, deep down, most girls would like to plan for, and be a part of, that familial trip to somewhere.

Figuring that if I wanted a full-family experience to call my own I would have to go out and find one, I did just that. I absolutely love to ski; so, when I heard that my cousin and her family were going skiing, I invited myself on their family trip. They were most gracious, and—as I like to tease—they allowed this old grey mare to tag along. As I had vacationed with this family of five before, I was certain we'd have a good time. An outing with them is as comfortable as putting on a pair of cozy, worn in slippers. When we are together, we laugh, tease, debate, and heckle. It's just all good.

Plans were made, schedules were matched, and at the appointed time we all successfully arrived at the slopes for a much-anticipated time of fun and frolic. Four within our party of six were relatively new skiers. My cousin and I were the veterans in the crew. Considering the ratio, I was horrified when my cousin's husband announced that we, as a family, would stick together at all times and at all costs. Figuring the edict was non-negotiable, I didn't breathe a word as he directed our entire group—which was a little wobbly to say the least—toward the massive lift that loomed ahead.

I gulped when we arrived. As I looked up at the six-person chair for which we were in line, I wondered if Mr. Togetherness really knew what he was asking. The chair lift drill resembles something akin to the way horses are lined up and placed into their gates before a race. When the lift operator gives the cue, the gates shoot open. At that point, skiers must frantically shuffle, in skis, to a line in the snow. There they must suddenly stop on a dime without incident, clear their poles, and catch the moving seat as it approaches from behind. When the chair hits the back of a skier's legs, they must immediately sit and calmly wait for the bar to lower and secure them in the chair. (Did I mention this is all to occur without incident?)

When the ski gates opened, our little band scrambled to catch our ride. Suddenly, the family member who had originally been in slot number one, somehow got discombobulated. Poles went flying in different directions and before we knew it, members previously in slots three, four, and five had all managed to change places in a matter of one point five seconds. When the snow flurries settled, I had no earthly idea where the six-year old in my charge had landed or how the teenager ended up sitting next to me.

Each member of our six, however, miraculously managed to locate and remain attached to the seat. But the rise to the top would not be without mild casualty. The six-year old's ski popped off mid-ride, falling to its untimely demise on the snow below. (I secretly thanked God it hadn't whacked and killed an unsuspecting downhiller!) Mostly, I was relieved that we managed to stick together (as ordered); but I was also thrilled that we had successfully continued up the mountain without loss of limb or sight of blood.

People usually ask what happened to the ski. I'm pleased to report that the lone stick was able to rejoin us via a gracious person who responded to our loud requests to, "Send up the ski!" The minute piece of equipment was placed on its very own chair and successfully rode all the way to the top where it was warmly greeted by our little motley crew.

When it was all said and done, my family agreed that ours was a perfect trip. So nice in fact that I wouldn't be surprised if we made a repeat performance somewhere in the unsuspecting Western regions. If we do that, however, we should probably call ahead and give the resort a heads up.

"ARE WE THERE YET?"

The people in my circle of friends are so kind to include me in their personal festivities and usually check-in to make sure I know the invitation to join them always stands. They call to see whether I have plans, and then remind me I am welcome in their homes. I'm so blessed to have such great relationships with such great people; but, even with their loving support, holiday situations can still leave a single gal in the dumps.

What I wasn't expecting or prepared for after one particular outing with my extended family was the twinge of depression I experienced when settling back into my routine. As I lounged on the couch drinking my coffee and going over the photos and videos from the trip, a profound reality hit me: I may never get to experience planning and enjoying my own family vacation. I was shocked by how much that thought hurt.

Many of us grew up anticipating the planning and trip-taking that comes with having a family car full of one's own clan. For many people, traveling to places like Washington D.C, Mount Vernon, Yellowstone National Park, and Mount Rushmore equals shared adventures of learning together. (You know what I mean—the family road trip where Mom encourages the kids in the backseat to "Look for a word that begins with "K," and dad points out the next historical marker?)

The fact that those trips have not yet materialized can be haunting. That's why my single friends and I have decided to gather a group of girls and take trips like this together. After all, in many ways, we are a family, too. While planning large-scale vacations can be a challenge, they're definitely worth it!

I am learning that it's probably a good idea to keep my thoughts regarding my lack of traditional family vacations to myself. I realized of late that non-single people, when listening to me complain, might feel that I'm suffering from something like "too-late remorse."

> *Single moms: Consider joining forces for a group road-trip. You'll definitely come home with some great stories!*

Here's what I mean. When we single gals watch other single girls go on reality shows designed to pair two unattached people, we don't generally have a lot of empathy. In our minds, they put themselves into a situation where twenty females vie for the attention of one man. *They certainly set themselves up for disaster,* we think. Then, when one contestant among the bunch routinely complains to her video diary that she has to compete for the lone man's affections, we say out loud to the television set, "You auditioned to be there, silly! You made the choice to parade your single self in front of the entire nation—if not the world for that matter. Hold tight, girl! Make it work!"

I might be off base on this one, but I am beginning to think that some who have families and marriages may, at times, view never-married or divorced singles in a similar light. Perhaps, they've decided that we wanted to be single. They feel that we got ourselves into this mess, and they're baffled by our intense desire to change our single status.

We single gals, however, see our plight as simply not yet having found our soul mates. We truly feel that we haven't come across the person with whom we want to wake up for the rest of our lives. We hear those words "until death do us part" and we take them seriously. If truth be told, we want to do life right.

I'm not saying we got it wrong by staying single. What I am saying is this: We are the first generation to grow up with divorce as a fairly normal and acceptable option. In response to that, we've done everything in our power to avoid taking that path. Maybe, we've been over-achievers to that end. While trying so hard to avoid divorce, we've actually managed to avoid marriage.

SO, WHAT'S A SINGLE GIRL TO DO FOR THE HOLIDAYS?

When you take all of these thoughts and feelings and questions, then mix in some holiday spirit, it isn't surprising to see how holidays can become the bane of the single humanoid. My family keeps hoping I will bring someone home for Thanksgiving dinner. Instead, I just keep bringing back the dog.

I'm reminded of a chat with Missy, the manicurist who works on my nails. Thirty-seven years of age, Missy has never been married.

"I saw a person this week, while I was home for Christmas, who I had not seen in the longest time," she reported while polishing my pinkie.

"Oh?" I asked.

"Yes," Missy nodded. "She is married but always seems unhappy when I see her. The first words out of her mouth to me were not 'Hey, Missy. How are you doing? How have you been? What have you been up to?' Nope. As soon as she saw me, she said, 'Are you still single?'"

I watched Missy's face fall as she shared. Why do people do that? I just don't know. But had I been in close proximity to the person who asked Missy that question, I would have taken an emery board to her nose!

Missy looked across the room and added, "I don't mean to complain, Stephanie. It's just that certain holidays … you know … like Christmas and birthdays? And sometimes Valentine's Day? They can be tough. Not always, but at times. I just … Well …"

"Yes," I replied as I gave her hand a squeeze, "I know."

Missy is a very positive, healthy-minded girl. She is no whiner. But that day, she voiced something only a single girl can grasp. To us, our lives are so much more than just our dating life or lack there-of. We have friends, activities, plans, goals, and dreams. We've conquered projects and earned awards. We've visited places and experienced adventures. We've seen amazing events, involved ourselves with important organizations and have met and spent time with extraordinary people. Sadly, however, folks sometimes want the latest scoop on our single status when they haven't seen us in a while more than they want to hear about our lives in general. Or, at least it can sure feel that way.

HAPPY BIRTHDAY TO ME

I once joked that I began celebrating my birthday in January and continued the festivities through September. After that, it was time to prepare for Christmas. These days, however, I just don't get as excited about birthdays as I used to. Maybe, that's because I can recall more than one birthday that I have spent alone.

Don't get me wrong. I'm not blaming anyone for that fact, and I have certainly enjoyed some amazing and exciting birthdays along the way. But I moved away from home in my late twenties, so celebrations with my family came to mean traveling about eight-hundred miles. While nearby friends sometimes graciously ask what I am doing for my big day and invite me out to dinner or a movie, or plan a quick gathering to celebrate, I've come to realize that the awkward thing about birthdays and the single gal is that it's no one's job to make sure she has a special day.

Thank goodness for family members with great memories! I am always amazed when my mom, grandmother, aunt, uncle, and cousins call to sing the birthday song to me. I still get tickled and am thrilled that my family keeps up the tradition. Their calls come sprinkled throughout the day and help to make the occasion all the more special. But I am sincere when I say that my expectations for the big day lower as I age.

I guess I've come to embrace a few realities: 1) It's no one's job to make my birthday special; 2) If the day is going to be happy, it's up to me to make it so; and 3) I better start making my b-day plans early, or it could prove to be a very lonely day.

I'll never forget one particular birthday when I was alone and another single friend insisted I join her for lunch. Sounded good to me, so I carved out the time and began looking forward to it. As the day dragged on, however, my friend kept postponing. By the time dinner rolled around, she was out of time and suggested that we meet at her cousin's house. I had never met her cousin, but the calendar was open and I appreciated that she was trying to include me. I stayed open to the plan.

When I arrived at the home of her sibling, however, I wished I'd politely declined. There I found my friend, her sister, and two squealing toddlers. Dinner became a quick-order from a nearby place that delivered to the house. And the evening passed slowly as the women yelled over the kids and chased after them. Thankfully, I found a way to make a graceful exit fairly early.

From that day on, I knew it was up to me to have a fabulous birthday. Since then, I've determined to make it happen. I try to create as many ways to enjoy my special day as possible. I ask myself what I'd like to do, and then I work to make sure it happens. Perhaps I want to lunch with a friend and spend the rest of the day relaxing. One year I even treated myself to a lovely evening at a fabulous hotel that featured a water and light show set to music while dinner was served. While I do choose to accept the celebratory invitation of a well-meaning friend at times, I have come to weigh my options first and choose what sounds best to me.

One friend of mine offered some thoughts on the birthday thing as well, "I use the day to reflect and recharge. If it's a work day, I call in sick!" Great advice if you ask me. So, here's to a great day of celebrating you. Make some plans and make sure it's special.

WEEKENDS WERE MADE FOR ...

The Saturday after I returned from that hilarious family ski trip, I quickly fell back into the groove of hunkering down on the couch and catching up on reality shows from the previous week. Those things are so addictive, and though a very guilty pleasure, I do find them oddly therapeutic. Watching other humans work out their issues before a stunned world brings a sort of calming effect to my life. I agree wholeheartedly with my friend Chloe who says, "[Reality TV] reminds me that I am not crazy. They are!"

On that particular Saturday, after I'd caught up on my shows, I tuned in to find it was "Family Day" on the Food Network.

"Ah, yes," I sighed aloud, "Total weekend therapy for a single girl just coming off of a family get-a-way."

Naturally, after an emotional week of realizing that my own personal family vacation might not materialize, you can imagine the "joy" I expereinced when the only thing on cable were two non-reality-television shows featuring happy families cooking together. Just what the lonely-hearted single needed on her only day off to recover from a ski trip with someone else's family!

In the first hour, I watched a mother and son gush over their family's recipes as they spent time together in the kitchen.

"Yeah, just dig that knife in a bit deeper," I hollered at the television set.

"No. Over here, Mama." I said getting a bit louder. "The single lady on the sofa in her bathrobe. Just a little more to the left. That's it. In the heart!"

I can't explain why I simply didn't change the channel and end the scene I was creating in front of my television, but I soon found myself engrossed in the following program as well. In the first segment, a married couple cooked their family's generational recipes. In the second, I watched as grandmothers and their daughters explained how the recipes they prepared had been passed down the family tree.

Somebody just take me out back and shoot me, I thought. *It's only 10:00 a.m., and I feel a martini calling my name!*

Of course, I'm kidding about that last part, but my heart wasn't doing so well by the time I'd endured two hours of someone else's happy-family-culinary-memory-making.

The following week wasn't much better. I was scheduled for my annual visit to the gynecologist. Don't you just love those? You get the wonderful opportunity to see pregnant women, sometimes with doting husbands in tow, going to learn the sex of their baby. I, on the other hand, sat waiting to get a tutoring session in menopause.

Shall I shout from the rooftops the trials of the single life? Probably not. My neighbors might call the police. But what's a single girl who finds herself in these hormone induced dilemmas supposed to do?

Here's my suggestion. Make chocolate chip cookies and eat the entire batch! Food channel, move over. Girlfriend is in the kitchen making cookie dough, and it might not even make it to the oven! Now that's what I call therapy.

My friend Missy came up with a tip that I simply must share as well. When you're at the Thanksgiving table this year and the focus on your dating life begins to affect your appetite, try this exit line: "Please excuse me, I have singleness. I'll call you when it's over."

Being single *is* our choice. It's true. We aren't interested in just taking whatever comes our way. We've signed up for the job so to speak. So, to the innocent onlooker, perhaps we *are* perceived as having received our just desserts.

"So be it," I say, "Pass the cheesecake, please. Oh, and add a bit more of that chocolate if you don't mind."

Grab a spoon and join me, won't you? I say, if we've got it, we might as well enjoy it while it lasts!

Chix Chat:

1. Describe your most recent family vacation or trip. Where did you go? Would you go on another outing with these people again?
2. If you could plan one incredible family vacation, where would you go and what would you do?
3. What are your favorite holidays? Which ones do you dread?
4. Describe your perfect weekend.
5. Brainstorm a list of ways to celebrate your next birthday. What would you really enjoy doing? What would make you feel special?

Chapter 7

When Your Pet is Your Kid

"His name is ... First Friend, because he will be our friend
for always and always and always."
—Rudyard Kipling

As I considered the topic of holidays in preparation for the previous chapter, my thoughts turned to one Thanksgiving when my cousin's droop-eared Basset Hound, Daisy, turned up missing. Right after we bowed our heads to give thanks and started to pass the sweet potatoes, someone noticed she had slipped the bonds of the back yard and had gone completely AWOL. The pampered pure breed was gone! Plates dropped and shoes flew as family members, ranging in age from six to sixty, dashed out the door leaving Grandma and Uncle Bill alone with the turkey and dressing.

I grabbed my keys and ran for the car as the gravel under my feet painfully reminded me that I had thrown off my high heels in the panic and was now completely barefoot. *If I have to go it on foot at some point, it will hurt; but I can stand it for a worthy cause,* I determined with my heart pounding. No way was I coming home without that dog.

My panic deepened as I realized we were near a busy road. I drove down the middle of the street, stopping Texas-sized Suburbans left and right. No one was going to pass by me without hearing about and sharing in our plight. "Find Daisy!" became the adopted mantra of Coles Crossing that Thanksgiving Day. Soon even the holiday-making neighbors were instructed in what to do should the slippery hound show up on their doorsteps.

In time I happened upon a couple taking their post stuffing stroll. They were pleased to share that they had indeed seen a brown and white flash heading "that way." With a relieved "thank you," I threw the car in reverse and tore in the direction of their pointing fingers. A few hundred yards up, to my amazement, I came across some kids chasing the Canine from Kansas down a driveway. (Apparently, she had been happily drifting from house to house until she saw me and dashed into warp speed ahead.) Daisy knew I had come for her, and the race was on.

"Follow that dog!" I hollered to the boys playing in the street. "I'll pay you!"

Three middle-school aged kids took the bait (though they didn't know I'd left my purse back in the house) and tore off in the direction of the pooch as I followed in my car. Daisy led—the three boys trailing closely behind her—while I in my four-runner tried to hurry, yet not flatten, them all. Ironically, the dog still outran us.

A puddle ended the pursuit. Daisy didn't want to get wet or dirty, so she came to an abrupt halt when water appeared in her path. I scooped up the fur ball and tossed her into the back seat, both of us panting. When I turned to slide into the front seat, six little hands greeted me, reaching out for their expected payment.

While they hadn't actually caught the dog, they had chased her, they were winded, and they deserved reward. It had been quite an adventure!

"Dig in," I sighed as I extended the plastic Tupperware bin full of quarters that I keep in the back seat for toll booths. "Whatever you can pull out with one hand is yours!"

Convinced they had completely hit the jackpot, they shoved their grimy human paws into the coinage and grabbed with all their might. I too felt like I had hit the lottery. In my possession was the prized pedigreed pooch. Now I could triumphantly return to the family table where we could truly all give thanks.

I, the odd-ball single, played hero for a day. Already far from home, the last thing my cousin, his wife, and their two toddlers needed was a missing family dog to add to the holiday stress.

In our family, pets are family, too. In fact, my aunt actually gives my dog an ornament with his name on it each year. He even has his own mini-Christmas tree!

Maybe you can relate to our family's wild determination to bring a pet safely home. Many animal lovers would, too. But I think a fellow single girl might understand better than anyone. Why? Because many of us singles, who don't have kids, have dogs. Or cats. Or birds and bunnies like my friend Sadie. Those pets become part of *our* unique, single family stories. A very important part.

While watching the ole telly the other day, I caught the end of a very popular reality show. (Can you tell I am into reality shows?) A particular contestant was thrown off of the proverbial island and prepared to pack her bags and head home. Suddenly, she launched into quite a descriptive homecoming that would include a long-awaited reunion with her cat. Now, I have to tell you, as much of an animal fanatic as I am (and that puts it mildly, just ask my mother), I began to squirm in discomfort as the grown woman expounded in great detail on her desire to get home to hold and snuggle with her cat. Honestly, it was a bit more than I could handle. I wanted to change channels out of embarrassment for her, but my hand was frozen on the remote.

To the outside world, to those who do not have a special bond with a pet, the woman's behavior is nothing short of strange. The non-pet people group just doesn't get it. I, on the other hand, kind of understand. And if you're still reading this chapter, I think you might, too.

> **Notice**: *If you don't have the pet thing going on in your life, you might not fully appreciate this chapter. If you want to jump ahead, that's okay. It will always be here for you when you do fall in love with an irresistible creature.*

HERE, FIDO!

Dogs as pets date back at least as far as the days of ancient Greece. One famous example, recovered from the rubble at Pompeii shows the shape of a dog stretched out next to a little boy's body. Two friends in life remain side-by-side in death for thousands of years after their passing. That just plain gets to me.

I've had several dogs in my lifetime. Baron Von Huffman, the attack dog. He bit me on my birthday!—was one of them; but "Judge, the wonder dog," came into my life when I was house hunting for my first home. In those days, I was determined to have a black Labrador Retriever by the time I moved. Labs run in our family, and I just couldn't live in that house all alone!

Knowing I was in the market for a puppy, a friend called to interest me in one Lab-mix she'd found. Her neighbor's dog had given birth, and she had hand-picked the male she thought was calling my name. I just had to take a look. The moment I saw the dog I knew he was for me. Judge was the first-born of the brood, coal black, and was everything I wanted.

Nothing like a puppy to keep you laughing and smiling! But, let me tell you, Judge and I had plenty of days when I thought I had reached the end of my rope with him. He dutifully shredded four grill covers and chewed through all of the railing on my entire deck. The black terror pulled trees out of pots, tore flowers out of planters, and stole the tin pans from my neighbor's garden. If that wasn't enough, he also managed to drag home Mr. Wiley's Sperry Top-Sider loafers and his back door rug to boot. Anything at mouth level was completely fair game to this pooch.

Judge's early days were obviously a bit stressful. In fact, I was convinced that one of us would not live to see his third birthday. We both, however, managed to survive; and I celebrated with a party and a cake. Friends brought their dogs and even went home with party favors in bags. (It was quite a "hoot" as they like to say in the South!)

WOMAN'S BEST FRIEND

Thankfully, Judge's days of destruction are behind him and he has turned into the most wonderful traveling companion. He has been on business and pleasure trips, even joining me on the reoccurring, eight-hundred-mile trek to see the family. Judge has stayed at a Hilton in a major city and numerous other hotels and motels. He has bounced along the beaches of the south, trotted along the hills and the rivers of Tennessee, flown on planes and ridden in cargo vans. He is a happy camper, and I think camping—in an RV—might even be something we take up next. No promises in regards to that idea. Merely speculation.

The fact is, I take "The Judge" everywhere. He loves to "go" (the magic word for most dogs), and he seems to think that going for a ride is his personal birthright. Not just an option.

One of our favorite trips is to Starbucks where he lounges at my feet at an outside table. "The Boy" holds court while passers-by praise his beauty and pat his nose. But he's not just another pretty face. He's also beginning to enjoy performing community service work.

JUDGE TO THE RESCUE

My neighbor Ann called recently to thank my dog for his help. You read that right. She called for Judge.

The previous week a huge ground hog had taken up residence under her backyard shed. It was the size of a small dog and would come out, sit on the grass, and peer around. What he did beneath the shed was the dreaded mystery. Was he burrowing holes to compromise the building's foundation? Was he planning to attack them in the night? Whatever it was, Ann didn't want to find out.

I offered to bring Judge over and take a look.

With her blessing I grabbed my morning coffee, got the leash, and headed across the street with the quadruped of choice. When we got to her backyard, Judge looked for the nearest hole in the fence while I worked to focus his attention on the shed. When he finally got the whiff he needed, he began the hunt. (Good thing the dog was too fat to squeeze under the structure or that ground hog would have been toast!) As Judge dug and sniffed, his furry black end wagged with the force of the movement. Once I figured the ground hog had been through enough trauma and would hopefully move on to new territory, I called off the hound and we retreated to our abode.

Ann called a few days later to let me know that the ground hog had, indeed, packed up and moved on. They had not seen him since Judge's little visit.

The dog did a good deed that week. Now he rests at my feet as I write, waiting for his next chance to save the day. My friend Gina says that Judge's work on the ground hog might lead to a great way to make some side money.

"Hey, if this catches on," she laughed, "you'll have to start charging for servicing the neighborhood!"

Not a bad idea. I think I'll go and print out some signs.

Forget the lemonade stand thing. How about, "Extermination: $25. Have dog, will travel"?

WHAT'S THAT ON THE MANTLE?

Not long ago I had dinner with a friend I'd not seen in ages. As we caught up over sushi, I asked for an update on her dog.

"How is Sasha?" I asked, remembering that the sweet critter was around before she and her spouse had their son. They considered Sasha their first "child."

Unfortunately, I learned that Sasha had gone on to the great grassy knoll in the sky, and my friend was doing the best she could to cope. The couple missed the dog terribly.

As we chatted, my friend shared that they had cremated Sasha and saved a curl from her tail. They had placed her ashes in an urn, which they kept on the mantle above the fireplace.

Sounded like good ideas to me.

Sasha's passing got me thinking about us gals and our non-human "kids." I wondered what I would do when the day of days finally arrives for Judge. As much as I pray for his health and long life, I know full well that Judge will not live forever. So, the question began to loom: What to do when he passes?

My friend Noel—the one who tells it like it is—suggested that I just get another dog. Noel recently adopted a huge white pup named Beau. Since then, she has contracted severe doggie love; and I'm not sure she'd go long without one at her side. Beau is an old codger, a lot like Judge, and can be found happily lying at her feet all hours of the day. Pet me, love me, feed me, walk me—sums up our boys' very reasonable demands. Noel and I agree that what we receive in return from our dogs is beyond measure.

> What we receive from our pets is beyond measure.

Our critters are there for us when we wake up. They are there waiting when we come home to our cold, dark houses. They are there when we go to bed, and they stay close when we feel so sick that we can't move. Judge is even with me when I run errands. In fact, he goes just about everywhere.

I recently joked to a friend. "I am praying that Judge lives to be fifty."

When her jaw dropped and she turned ash white, I assured her I was kidding.

But part of me was serious!

I once mentioned the "ashes" possibility to my mother. She seemed horrified.

"You know, cremation?" I muttered, hoping she'd see the value in it.

Instead, she continued to look stunned, remarking as she patted my hand: "Now, don't get carried away."

Judge has been my best friend and roommate for a long time now. I have lived alone with him for *years*. I can't just walk away and forget about my furry friend when he crosses over. He deserves a proper burial and a special place to be laid to rest.

Recently, Noel discovered that a church in our area created an impromptu pet cemetery on their property. I was quite surprised and, truthfully, relieved by this news.

"Wow, that would be perfect." I said with a sigh. "I could so do that."

A part of me that had been pondering that "what to do then" question rested that night. There truly is a God in heaven, seeing my needs, loving me, hearing my heart, and helping me plan. He knows what matters to me. He created my dog and brought him to me. And as always, He will help me take care of every dilemma—even if it's the passing of a precious pup. Thus, I think I found a resting place for "The Judge." We shall see.

President Harry S. Truman once famously said, "If you want a friend in Washington, get a dog."[1] I say, every single gal should seriously consider adopting a pet. And if you already have one or two—know that it's okay to think about their futures. It doesn't hurt to dabble a bit and consider a plan for the days to come. Know your options. You'll be glad you did.

And now, if you'll excuse me, Judge and I have a much-needed date with my laptop and a latte. Who knows, we might even run into the cute guy in the Mercedes who owns Ava the Great Dane!

Chix Chat:

1. Describe your pet and share his or her name.
2. What arrangements do you make for your pet when you need to be away? Do you kennel the pet or do you enlist sitters?
3. How does your family refer to your pet?
4. If you could travel anywhere with your pet, where would you go and what would you do?
5. Do you have plans for when this pet goes to heaven? Explain.
6. In the event you were unable to care for your pet due to circumstances beyond your control, who could step in to help? Does that person have easy access to your home? Have you made the proper introductions between pet and fill-in caretaker? If not, give that person a call or e-mail today to set up a meeting.
7. If you don't have a pet, but have been thinking about adopting one, talk with a friend whose pet seems to fit your lifestyle and needs. She'll be happy to share with you the joys and routines of pet ownership, while also giving helpful tips that can point you in the right direction. Plan to chat with her this week.

Chapter 8

Travel Well, Travel Right

"It's not where you go, it's who you're with."
— *Unknown*

I love to travel—and just so you know—I do travel without my dog sometimes. I travel as much as I can. And except for the post 9/11 airport culture, I enjoy it. At one point in my life, my job had me on the road so much I found that I was becoming more comfortable in an airport than at home. Thankfully, those days have passed. These days, I prefer to travel for leisure.

When I was a little girl, my grandparents whisked me away on exciting tours across the Western states. I guess that might be the reason I contracted the travel bug early. I remember impatiently looking out the window for their RV, anxiously waiting for it to pull into our driveway. I couldn't wait for our latest adventure to begin!

I just knew that, when I grew up, I would be a traveling kind of gal. I looked forward to it so much—and for some reason sincerely believed my future so depended on it—that I actually used to practice packing and unpacking my tiny white rectangular suitcase with the slim red trim. Oh, the places I would go!

It was so exciting!

Years ago I collected articles on what to pack and how to pack efficiently. Now I just Google the latest tips or collect them from friends. One great idea came from my friend, Cheryl.

"I always save out one outfit and put it in a Ziplock™ bag. I keep it on the bottom of my suitcase and save it for the return flight," she declared. "On the last day of the trip, when I open that bag, it has that scent of home; and I soon forget the smell of the location I am leaving."

Cheryl is a seasoned world traveler. Mud huts and earthworms do not frighten her one bit. Starting up a school in an exotic location or buying a cow or two for a village is just a part of who she is and what she does. She even survived cancer as a single woman, and I highly suggest her book—*Six Foot Tall and Bald*—to every single girl (See Resources section for more information).

Many of us girls crave adventure and pride ourselves in thinking that we have the ability to take off and experience the world. But as Cheryl relayed to me after her latest adventures in Madagascar, "Traveling is not for the weak at heart. Some of us just do better in a five-star hotel."

My mind drifted from our conversation for a moment as I recalled past group trips that truly drove that point home.

JUST NOT CUT OUT FOR THE ROAD

We single gals are traveling more and more these days. And since many of us don't have family members to travel with, we team up with like friends and head out on those dream trips once kept on the back burner.

I am fortunate to have experienced quite a few outings with a wide array of friends. Most of the time, the jaunts are great and everyone gets along. But to be completely honest, on certain trips I'm tempted to take the next taxi home.

One particular weekend away, years ago, I found myself asking, "Just who invited who on this trip anyway?" That vacation produced some interesting personality clashes. Unfortunately, it didn't dawn on me until after the trip was underway that I should have studied the guest list long before we launched. I was so excited to get time away with friends that I forgot one very basic premise: know thy travel mates.

With luggage packed and water bottles filled, four other single gals and I began to load into our van. Suddenly, one of the girls announced that she would ride in the front. Apparently, she got carsick and would therefore be entitled to that prime space for the duration of our travels. This came as a shock to two or three other girls in our group who also struggled with motion issues. Needless to say, we all dug into our purses and promptly passed around the Dramamine.

On another trip, the sleeping arrangements weren't exactly what one weary traveler had in mind. When we arrived at our sleeping quarters, everyone scattered and settled in. Evidently, the bed that Sue landed was not up to her standards.

That's all we heard about the entire trip: "That bed hurts my back." "Have you ever had a worse night's sleep?" "Oh, my spine!"

Been there, done that, bought the t-shirt, right? Oh, the stories we single travelers could tell!

I once joined a traveling party that ended up with a self-appointed Cruise Director calling the shots! This vacation had nothing in common with *The Love Boat*'s pleasant excursions. One overly organized member of our crew made it clear that being together was "just better." According to her, no one was to do anything outside the group. She felt it wasn't right. It wasn't as much fun; and supposedly, it was not appropriate.

Really? Since when? I privately mused.

I must confess that I have the type of personality that requires me to sometimes pull back from groups when I need to recharge my batteries. I know that concept is completely foreign to you social butterflies out there, but some of us girls are just designed this way.

Imagine the tension that grew as I found my relaxing vacation turning into a well-planned event! I seriously considered getting "accidentally" lost in the woods that week, but the thought of prowling, hungry bears got the best of me.

FOR THE GOOD OF THE ORDER

Let's face it. A trip can be great. But only if everyone involved gives it her best. In defense of the all-for-one and one-for-all travel mentality, a refresher course now and then on how to weigh our personal expectations against those of our travel mates is not a bad idea. Everyone goes into a vacation with a different concept of what "a good time" and "rest" look like and actually mean. Sometimes, we just won't all agree on their definitions.

I may sound like my mother here, but think about it: We singles get so excited about getting away, and having someone to go away with, that it's easy to forget the obvious step of considering our compatibility with our travel buddies. Also, it never hurts to revisit as a group the Golden Rule (do unto others as you'd like them to do unto you). Imagine if we all openly discussed our hopes, needs, and personal preferences before heading out. Wouldn't that help make sure everyone has a good time?

If truth be told, we singles don't always realize how we come across when we are out of our routines, our controlled environments, and our personal comfort zones. Remember, we don't have someone there to say, "It drives me crazy when you…" or "I'd really rather you didn't …"

I want to vacation, and I want to be a part of a group; but I know it's healthy to remember that it takes work from all parties involved in order to make a shared time away a success. We all know a great trip doesn't just happen. It requires a car full, bus full, or plane-aisle full of people who have prepared and plan to get along.

Given enough time and a few stressful situations, people can and will irritate each other. It's only natural. My idiosyncrasies will get on your nerves, and yours will probably get on mine. If we're not aware and sensitive to each other's needs, however, someone is bound to feel miserable. And nobody wants trouble when in paradise.

> *All parties must work together to make a shared time away a success.*

I once took a trip with a gal who could get really grouchy. For some reason, she had the idea that people were supposed to stop what they were doing and cheer her up during these episodes. It took everything within me not to say, "Hey, if you're that tired, dismiss yourself for a nap!" And too, she would suddenly hole herself up in seclusion. It left me scratching my head wondering why she even bothered to come along.

These little stories are good reminders that how we come across as a whole, how we handle the accommodations and the situations that arise, and how we treat other traveling companions can determine our current and future invitations. If we aren't getting as many invites as we used to, it just might be time to revisit past experiences and make needed adjustments. (Oops. Did I say that?)

I once traveled with some people who stayed out until 2:00 a.m. every morning and then slept in until 11:00 a.m. the next day. This approach to life was just was not my style, and I really couldn't adjust to it. In retrospect, I realize I shouldn't have gone on a trip with them; but I did and learned a big lesson. In the end, they were frustrated; and we all wished I'd just stayed at home in my jammies watching reruns on TV. While they were looking forward to the nightlife and the party scene, I had been mapping out the shops and historic home tours. I now better understand the importance of talking through the "entertainment" factor before purchasing the plane tickets.

On the other hand, some personal preferences can be laid aside more easily than others. I'm reminded of the time Dharma joined us for a trip to the beach.

She should have reconsidered the entire thing and stayed home as well. She had a list of dietary issues that required more time in the specialty food stores than in the cafés. I must say, it's just a complete drag to want to down French fries and Cokes™ while one lone person in the group will not rest until you have hunted down her wheat grass.

It doesn't hurt to have a few travel tips in mind as you plan your next adventure. Remember that vacationing requires an investment of our time and our money. We have every right to be careful in whom we invest our precious resources.

In the end, traveling with a group means taking a trip with people. And those other people will have hopes and expectations that need consideration. It's easy to say, this is *my* trip, and I have found myself doing that on more than one occasion. But the older I get and the more I roam, the more I appreciate these simple travel tips. They stretch me. And I am amazed at what a nice person I can be when I crawl outside my "box."

To prove that I truly do take my own advice, I want to share one last tale. A new girl accompanied my friends and me on a spring fling. I knew I needed to get to know her better, so I was determined to use that time away to invest in her. I did. And it was fabulous.

I will admit, however, that we both got off on the wrong foot our first day out! She made a wise crack, and I snapped back. Immediately, I knew what I'd done and became acutely aware that we had a full few days left ahead of us. Unfortunately, she was an "activity person" and I, a "napper." But in spite of those differences, I determined to make it work.

We still get together and chat. She's been a wonderful help to me many times since—a great reminder of the good that comes when we travel well and travel "light."

I ran these travel suggestions by my friend Tiffany, a PhD who has quite the analytical mind. I could see the wheels turning as she mulled over my notes.

"The empirical data is clear, Stephanie," she announced with a familiar gleam in her eye. "What we single girls need is a Travelling Companions Matching Service."

I started to laugh as she began to pitch the idea: "Please visit our website and locate the Travel Survey. You will find it available in an easy to download format. Please allow an hour for completion. Once you have submitted your form online, should your application be approved, you will be notified of your acceptance and matched accordingly."

I think that girl may just be on to something.

Chix Chat:

1. If you've ever been on a trip with your single friends, describe it. If not, consider where you'd like to go and who you'd take along for a group trip.
2. Describe the best trip you've ever taken. Who went with you?
3. What could you work on or change about you to make the next trip even better?
4. Name one thing you would avoid doing on your next trip. What do you want to be sure happens on your next trip?
5. If preparing for an upcoming vacation, consider sharing this chapter with your travel mate(s) before you go. Consider encouraging your group to create its own travel survey!

CHAPTER 9

Home Sweet Home

"You have too much stuff."
— Mom

THUS are the words I hear about once a year from my mother's lips as she reminds me that I have too many things. I definitely wish I'd inherited her freedom from the need for stuff. In fairness to my mom, I've always been a bit of a pack rat. And I knew it drove her crazy. I can remember waking up one Saturday to find my mother out in the driveway holding a garage sale featuring some of my treasures! Another time, I had a complete meltdown when she threw out my green cardboard masterpiece that displayed glued elbow macaroni. I mean, really, how could she? Everyone knows we're supposed to save that kind of stuff!

THERE'S NO PLACE LIKE HOME

We girls have to put our things someplace. The obvious solution is to create more storage space. But once you've bought every possible gadget and bin from the organization store and your home still seems to split at the seams, you realize you're outgrowing your space. The thought of a bigger home starts to loom, and you soon succumb to looking for that next place of residence. But where to begin? A bigger rental? A condo? A loft? A house? I feel like I'm in the thirty-one flavors ice cream store. The options are truly overwhelming.

Have you ever noticed how certain books for women (fiction or non) usually feature a single gal that resides in an apartment building with a doorman? Now, I have to tell you, I have lived in both California and Tennessee, and at no point did I ever see doormen. Of course, they weren't common when lived in the barrio with two other classmates in L.A. But I'm not sure that most women in

Wyoming or Texas or Maine or Kansas necessarily run into them either. It seems to me that the doorman scenario usually applies to those who are currently sans spouse and living on the ritzy side of Manhattan. Most of us single gals—at least those I know—don't generally land the glamorous apartment featuring a cute doorman. We're content to simply find a comfortable nest to call home.

At some point, I decided that me and my stuff needed a new place to reside. Even before I made the decision to begin house hunting, I started collecting items that would go in my future home. Like a grill. It sat on my apartment's deck for at least a year—even though grills weren't even allowed in our units! Soon my space was overloaded with things that wouldn't fit the square footage of my studio.

Once I had a job with a solid paycheck, it seemed that I shouldn't throw my money away on rent each month. (Or, at least, that was what I had come to believe.) More than that, I'd escaped the housing market of California and was stunned to find that home ownership was actually a possibility in my new locale. I excitedly jumped at the chance.

LOCATION, LOCATION, LOCATION

During my apartment dwelling days, the choice of where to live was determined by what I could afford. Sure, location and neighborhood were considered; but when you're only bringing home a few hundred dollars or so a month—as was my case—your options have to match the cash flow. I hoped my search through the housing market would allow me to be more discriminating about where I would and would not live. But I soon learned that my taste in locale still did not exactly match my budget.

My real estate agent was a fabulous person and friend. I trusted her, and I felt that the scary leap into the land of mortgages would be much easier with her by my side.

Before we started the process, I did my homework and was quite proud of my discoveries. "Okay. Areas one, two, and ten, are where I'd like to end up," I stated confidentially. "I am definitely not interested in area seven."

"Well," my very professional realtor responded, "all you can afford are these." She held out her hands and smilingly suggested that I scan the sheets before me. To my sheer disbelief, ninety percent of them were in dreaded area seven.

When I started my house hunt, buyers worked off "white sheets." These were printed pages of information a realtor provided from her agency's computer system. These sheets included a list of homes for sale, but many times offered little more than a house's price and location. Nowadays, people can shop from the comfort of their own homes, enjoy virtual tours of each and every room, and even scan the neighborhood via tools like Google maps!

I noted first the pages featuring the properties that met my price point and those with my have-to-have criteria. As the search got underway, I traipsed through a myriad of subdivisions and side roads trying to be positive as I went. *It's close to work. It has lots of nice trees.*

When I first drove past the home that would one day become my own, the trees were in full foliage. The street was everything I had hoped for, and the lush green yard called my name. The house wasn't located in the areas that had once topped my list, but I still remember gleefully whispering, "Wow, that place could really be mine." When we finally set up an appointment to see the inside, I exclaimed, "This house just makes me happy!" Windows all around let light in from all points of view. Hardwood floors lay beneath the new carpet, and the deck out back begged me to spend hours of fun with friends, happily grilling away our weekends at my place.

I soon signed a stack of paperwork transferring the home to my name and moved in with the help of thirteen fabulous people from my church. The clouds broke open and a torrential downpour ensued, but coffee and the Krispy Kreme™ donuts helped to ease some of the pain. To this day, I am overwhelmed and more than grateful for the kindness they showed in moving me. I now look back and laugh. I was so excited to show them my new digs, yet I made sure to drive them past the nicest houses on the route to my new address. I wasn't moving to area one, two, or ten, but I could at least take them on the scenic tour and make it, sort of, look like I did.

Forty-five minutes after everyone pulled up in front of my new home, the moving truck was empty. Everything sat in its appointed room waiting to find its place. I ordered tons of fried chicken with all of the fixings for lunch; we devoured every last crumb, and then they were gone. It had all happened so fast!

As I stood alone—just me, my stuff, and the un-mowed lawn—I could not have fathomed the hours and money I would soon pour into this exciting and new "investment." Deep in the heart of area seven.

MOVIN' ON UP

Overnight, I went from a small one bedroom apartment to a house with twenty-six-hundred square feet. The lot supposedly came in at about one-third of an acre.

But I was up for the challenge. As a new homeowner, I was determined to be the next Martha Stewart. (Remember, I have four sets of china, two sets of silver, and enough kitchen tools and appliances to help feed an army.) My hopes and dreams were piled just as high as my boxes, and I couldn't wait to dive in and go to work. Looking back now, I realize that, prior to signing the dotted line that said the house belonged to me, I had no idea what I was getting myself into.

Before I knew it, I was scrubbing floors, painting walls, replacing doors and windows—which also required treatments—repairing pipes, sealing walkways and a deck, trimming shrubs, enlisting the help of a plumber and an electrician, adding an alarm system, and repairing the fence. I slowly came to realize that, besides being a full-time career girl, I'd now added one of the most historic professions of all time to my name as well—that of housewife. (Meaning that I might as well have been married to my house for all the loving care it needed and the attention it would require.)

My house has two levels. It's not new, and I'm beginning to believe that it was the actual inspiration for the 1980's hit movie, *The Money Pit*. It sits in an older, established part of town, and most of my neighbors are retired. (I know. You're thinking, "You're kidding? How do you expect to meet a man there?" But they are home all day, they watch my house like hawks, and I love how very safe their diligence makes me feel!)

Owning a house is a joy and a privilege, even if it is a lot to take on. Add the responsibility of a day job, a personal and social life, and a girl's schedule can get pretty full.

In time I learned to deal with the taxes, insurance, and mortgages just like couples do. Then there were the countless home improvement decisions. Big ones. Like "Tile or linoleum?" "Hardwood or carpet?" For the single gal, one of the perks regarding those dilemmas is that they are somewhat simplified. Basically, we have no one to argue with over our choices, and that can be nice. My dog won't exactly chime in and say, "You should have gone with the gold veined tile, Stephanie."

My house is not for everyone. But it's mine. And it makes me smile. As one government official recently commented in an interview I caught while whizzing past the television set, "You don't need luxury to be happy." Hmm. I think I agree. At least there's a lot of happy going on at my place. The luxury part? Not so much.

My residence is not a Manhattan penthouse, nor is it on the pricier side of the tracks. But I'm okay with that. In fact, I get the biggest kick out of shopping in the higher end stores across town. When I do, they always ask for my zip code as I check out. I chuckle and think, *You really don't want to know.* But I give it, and they quickly tap in the first three digits. It's when I give them the last two numbers that I see them look up and slowly "tap-tap" the digits.

My home may not be the Taj Mahal; but when my friends come over, there's plenty of room. My space is quiet and it works. I refer to it as my sanctuary. My mom calls it the "B & B." A girl really can't ask for more.

ARE YOU READY TO JUMP?

Most of my single girlfriends in their late thirties have also taken the domestic and financial leap of homeownership—whether by buying a house, condo, or townhome. Some haven't.

Sheila, for instance, always told me she wouldn't buy a home while she was single. "That," she said, "is something you do with your spouse." Well, we are now past the forty-year mark; and I am wondering if at this point she might reconsider. I think she'd find it worth her time, money, and effort; but we shall see.

A twenty-six-year-old gal I knew purchased her first home. I was thrilled for her, but so amazed. I didn't own my first home until I was thirty-five. And at that point, I thought I was doing great! It's exciting to see the younger gals willing to make the investment as they are able. I say, "Good for them!"

I recently found myself asking that nagging question: why do so many of us feel the need to add a mortgage and a lawn to our already full solo plates? Maybe it's the maternal, homemaker instinct that causes us to seek the June Cleaver lifestyle. I will never know. But apparently the need for a home—our own home—is just in us. We dream of what the future could hold. Perhaps in buying a place, we prove that we are qualified and ready for whatever that future may bring. Maybe, we do it out of the need to invest wisely. I'm sure it's a bit different for each of us, but the fact remains: most of us love the thought of creating our very own, do-what-you-want-to-it, space.

THE YARD

I forgot that in buying a house I'd also get a yard. Well, make that two yards. A big one in the front and one in the back. My mother humorously refers to my front yard as the National Park. I refer to the back as merely "The Weeds."

When looking for a house, I wasn't thinking about the fact that I had contracted acute asthma the previous season. I wasn't exactly built for gardening anymore. But something within me sees yard work as a challenge. When I first moved in, I was determined to do the mowing myself—even in one hundred degree weather and matching humidity. These days, I do still mow the back weeds, as it only takes fifteen minutes. I used to give the front the old college try as well, but I eventually gave up the task to professionals and never looked back.

> *Most love the thought of creating our very own, do-what-you-want-to-it, space.*

While working from my home office, I began noticing that my neighbors would sneak out of their houses to feed and mow their lawns right after my lawn service worked their magic. My retired male neighbors watched what my lawn guy did, then hauled out their own mowers and matched my grass length. I even saw them head out to the store to buy fertilizer or pre-emergent, after they'd taken notes while peeking out their living room blinds.

They must be so proud of the money they save as the single gal next door shells out cash for a scene that they can reenact themselves. I've decided I am their little lawn blessing. Their landscape angel, if you will. And I'm pleased to admit: those lawns are looking pretty good if I do say so myself.

IT'S A GOOD THING?

When I purchased the house "as is" it didn't compute that I would pour my precious dollars into repairs, maintenance, and upkeep. For the record, when my sink clogs, I either fix it myself by heading out to the nearest home improvement store or I call the plumber and pay the three figure invoice. When a room needs painting, I either do it myself or hire it out. The decisions and the to-do lists are endless.

I was sitting on my deck one day watching Judge stalk and chase squirrels, when I noticed the rain gutters. They were loaded with leaves and gunk. The sides were all green. *Ooo!* I thought to myself. *Time to get those cleaned and scrubbed.*

While I could pay to have it done, I will carve out an hour or two, haul out my bright yellow ladder, put on the rubber gloves, fill the bucket with solution, sweep the gutters out, and get the job done. I don't mind it, though I'd rather spend my time doing other things. (Like shopping.) I remind myself that the exercise is great, that I enjoy being outdoors, and (in reality) it's good for me. It keeps me hip in that Martha sort of way, don't you think? Do-it-yourself upkeep is definitely a good thing. At least that is what I keep telling myself.

My list never gets shorter, but I love my home: One project at a time, one hour at a time, one hundred dollar bill at a time.

Owning your own home can and should be a girl's dream. Rest assured, it doesn't have to be a single gal's nightmare! If you're considering buying a home, do it. But I will tell you that if I were to do it all over again, I might look for something newer that required a lot less maintenance. (And I bet I'd look into options featuring adorable doormen, too.).

Chix Chat:

1. What area of town do you live in and what circumstances led you to that choice?
2. Ideally, would you like stay where you are or move?
3. If you were to purchase, would you choose a house, condo, or townhome? Why?
4. What needs to happen before you make that next move? What are you waiting for?
5. Take the time to assess your cash flow and do-it-yourself abilities prior to looking at property. For instance, do you enjoy yard work? If not, are you willing to take on lawn care and maintenance costs?
6. Would you enjoy painting and redecorating, or would you prefer a place more move-in ready? Explain.
7. Make a list of have-to-haves. Rank them in importance.

Part 3

When Life Happens

Chapter 10

What Doesn't Kill You ...

"If life's a bowl of cherries, then what am I doing in the pits?"
—Erma Bombeck

IT'S one thing to have to take out the trash, change out the light bulbs, or walk and feed the dog. It's a completely different matter when life places a collect call, and a single girl's the only one there to accept the charges. I've come to find that, when life and personal crises come to call, they are uninterested in my current status; and they are no respecters of persons. No matter what you say, no matter who you are, you just can't put "life" on hold.

Responsibilities. We single gals have a lot of them. House. Career. Social and personal lives. But when we deal wit the married set, things can get a bit tricky. If you're a single mom, sometimes you have to start and leave work early for the benefit of your child; and people at work might understand. But for those of us who don't have children, another standard reigns. Unless a single girl calls in "dead," people at work just can't imagine why she is unavailable to handle whatever they require.

One specific example comes to mind. It was girls' night out at the movies. When Lucy caught up with us at the box office, she breathlessly begged, "Please don't throw me off the island, girls!"

As she gasped for air, we all froze in hopes that she'd suddenly landed a last minute date!

"My boss," she continued in a rush, "said I either cancel my plans tonight or bring an out of town client with me. He's on his way. Here. Now!"

Luckily the client was male, unattached, and very adorably New York. In the end, his joining us was not a problem at all. But I was dumbfounded. I wondered whether or not Lucy's boss would've so imposed on her if she were married. Probably not.

Few people realize the added stress a single girl carries regarding expectations at the office, life after hours, and the needs of her aged parents or grandparents who may solely rely on her for help.

One year "life" punched my number and kept me on speed dial.

CALL FOR YOU ON LINE ONE!

It all began in the early days of summer. I'd just exited the auditorium from an all day conference, when I realized I'd better check my voicemail. Having been in non-stop meetings and presentations, I could only imagine the number of messages waiting for me. Though a half dozen required attention, I only recall one: "Ms. Huffman, this is the nurse at Sterling Inn. We wanted to let you know that your grandfather came downstairs today and asked us to call 9-1-1. He's in the emergency room. He appears to have pneumonia."

For years I'd anticipated the call, sometimes wondering how and when it would come. My grandfather was nearing ninety-five and lived alone in a lovely, independent living center. His wife, my grandmother, had died four years prior. Gramps—as I called him—was as lucid and fun as they came; yet I'd long recognized he'd eventually grow frail.

It was easy to want to spoil the man who had nursed my grandmother for five years before collapsing from the effort and placing her in an Alzheimer's unit. Sadly, the couple had outlived all of their children. Three had died at birth. My father, their first born, was the only child to survive to adulthood. Tragically, he died at thirty-six. That left them with just me; their only grandchild.

As I hung up the phone, my mind swirled. Where to begin? Whom to contact first? What to do with the house? The job? The dog? Is this the end of the road for my grandfather? Questions and logistics raced through my brain as my heart began to pound.

The reality that I was the sole immediate family member for this aging senior citizen hit me full force. I had prepared for this possibility for years, but I don't think I could've ever been completely ready for what lay ahead. (Many of you may never encounter this type of situation. This, however, was my lot.) In the back of my mind, I'd always hoped that, when this day came, I'd be married to a man who would help me in the process. But, alas, I was still single and needed to, not only oversee a host of Gramps' needs in California, but hold down my full-time job back in Tennessee, too.

Good thing I couldn't tell the future, for had I known what bizarre adventures the next three months would bring, I probably—much like Jonah in the Bible—would have taken a ship headed the opposite direction!

RISING TO THE CHALLENGE

When I arrived at the hospital, Gramps was not doing well. During his eight day stay, I rotated between sitting at his bedside and orientating to my situation. I needed to take over his personal business and finances, figure out and pay his bills, make certain his will was in order, and prepare his apartment for his future care. All these duties were crammed between e-mails and calls into work.

As tough as it was to be alone, I realized that not having siblings was a blessing. While I was not an expert in geriatric care and was sometimes unsure about what I was doing, no family member could point out my mistakes or disagree with my decisions.

I rode a learning curve as Gramps rested in the hospital and I tried to figure out how to help. Questions regarding insurance, nursing homes, home-health care, assisted living options, medications, and doctor's visits screamed for my attention. In the midst of that stress, I was shocked to find myself in an unexpected battle with the medical staff. They continually refused to inform me of his condition. I had no idea as to what tests he had undergone or what medications he took. I just kept asking myself, "Can they really withhold information from his only family?" It was so surreal!

Over and over again I heard, "You will have to speak to the doctor."

How frustrating to find myself in the position of trying to care for a patient whose status was a mystery! The hospital staff claimed that the HIPAA Law (Health Insurance Portability and Accountability Act) prevented them from answering my questions. But I held in my hands my grandfather's own release of information signed in their presence, his Power of Attorney, and his will. Why wouldn't they budge an inch? It was as if I was in a very bad dream. One from which I could not wake up.

Not knowing the doctor's schedule, it was difficult to know when to catch him. I did my best, but I was soon exhausted. Frightened. Alone. And weary of the battle.

The staff continually ignored my granddad's complaints that he couldn't breathe. For eight days, he lay struggling to catch any breath. Back at his apartment, after his release, I pulled out my own personal nebulizer (which I carry due to an asthma condition) and pumped him full of so much albuterol that at one point, he couldn't hold his own coffee cup due to the shakes. He could, however, breathe!

I wondered why the doctors and nurses remained so deaf to his cries, and my frustration grew. I figured the hospital had simply seen an elderly man. Alone. Helpless. Maybe they assumed it would only be a matter of time before he died. Why put out a lot of effort on his behalf? That's how it seemed to me. It was infuriating to say the least.

For four days, I nursed Gramps alone. It was a bit of a comedy of errors at times as I was certainly no Nurse Nightengale. But he was a trooper and worked hard to keep up his humor and spirits despite my limited abilities. The staff at his living community and one nurse did pop in to check on us, offering what they could from time-to-time. But for the most part, I was on my own.

"You're a brave man," I'd tease Gramps, referring to my lack of nursing skills.

"Wouldn't have it any other way," he'd respond with a wink.

Meals were delivered to his room for him, but feeding myself fell to me. Rest was not something either of us got during those days. The poor man could not sleep, and so we were up around the clock. In time, it got the best of me.

One day my cell phone rang just as I dozed off for a nap. I tried to process the name on the caller ID, but my brain couldn't compute through the fog. I picked up anyway. *It might be work,* I thought.

"You have been on my mind, Stephanie," came the voice of a friend. "I felt the need to call."

Cheryl had no idea what I was going through as we had not connected for a while. But that did not stop me from unloading on her listening ears. I felt so grateful for what I definitely believed was a Divine Appointment.

Gramps' health improved in a few short days, but that didn't mean I could return to business as usual.

"Well, Jim," the doctor said while slapping my grandfather's file closed, "I don't think you should live alone."

That haphazard statement suddenly became a mandate that I take him home to Tennessee. The thought of getting Gramps—who was almost bed ridden—through security and airports sent me scrambling for other options. As the panic set in, I kept telling myself there was time. He still had a bit of rehab to finish.

As he worked to regain strength, I worked to hold down my day job which was two thousand miles away. Neither the hospital nor Gramps' apartment had wireless service available for my laptop, so I had to sneak out to a little coffee place a few streets away. I was grateful that I was able to connect to their Wi-Fi and check e-mails—even if it meant sitting in their parking lot at eleven at night or six in the morning.

Once I'd made certain the home health and the assisted living services were in place, I drove down to Los Angeles for a business trip that had been scheduled months prior. The conference fell during my birthday week, and I was pleased to learn that, as an attendee, I'd be staying at the gorgeous Bonaventure Hotel. (I privately believed it was a secret birthday gift from heaven to me.) Even better, I was able to connect with a friend living in Santa Barbara. We met for lunch at my favorite place on the coast, and it was just what the doctor ordered! (A trip to the water has long been my favorite form of therapy. Nothing like sitting with my toes in the sand while chasing a seagull away from my takeout!)

While on business, I regularly called my grandfather to check in on him. Yet with each call, I could tell that he was not getting better, but worse. All of the progress we'd made together seemed to disappear.

After the conference, I raced to be with him and landed a four-hundred dollar traffic ticket in the process. In addition, I'd contracted a nasty cold and didn't want to jeopardize his fragile health. I could not continue to stay in the apartment with him, but the nurses at The Inn understood. They adored my very popular grandfather, and so—knowing he was in loving and capable hands—I boarded a plane back to Nashville. There, for the next ten days, I nursed myself back to health and wondered just how long Gramps had left.

A little over a week later, hospice phoned to let me know that my grandfather had gone into deep breathing and was no longer responding. He was very close to the end. It had been hard to fly home and leave him, and I questioned myself endlessly. The surprise message I received from a pastor, however, helped to ease my mind.

"Stephanie, I wanted to let you know that I was able to spend time with your granddad in prayer during those last hours," he said reassuringly.

I knew then that is the way Gramps would have it. I had strongly suspected that, if I stayed with him, my granddad would fight hard not to die. Not to let life go in front of me. And so things had worked out. If I could not be there when he passed, at least some other comforting and peaceful presence could.

Interestingly, I had experienced a nagging feeling that very afternoon to go out on my deck and just be alone. I kept getting side-tracked, but the call to go outside would not let up. Knowing my grandfather's life hung in the balance, I finally obeyed.

"I'm so sorry, Gramps," I whispered toward the trees in the backyard.

I didn't know if I was apologizing for the running political fights we'd managed to get into over the years or the fact that his life had been so sad. But for whatever reason, those words needed to be said. Somehow, they relieved me. Of what, however, I wasn't exactly sure. When the call came that my grandfather's spirit had indeed left the earth, I calculated and recalculated the time. I soon realized he passed away almost exactly when I "spoke" to him on the deck. It was one of those moments you can't explain and don't forget.

Gramps and I were buddies. I adored that man. In retrospect, I think ours was a fitting good-bye for a very strong, independent gentleman.

DECISIONS, DECISIONS, DECISIONS

With my plan in place, I loaded up the car with my luggage and the dog and began the trek to Texas. The state became my home-base for the next six to eight weeks. Judge stayed there with my mother while I finalized my grandfather's life. The last thing I needed was a five-figure kennel bill awaiting my return home, so I was grateful for Mom's willingness to keep the grand-dog.

When I arrived in California a few days later, it was late on a Friday afternoon. Before me lay the task of meeting with the funeral home; selecting a casket; deciding what suit my grandfather should wear; preparing the funeral, which I wrote and officiated as no pastor was available; contacting would-be attendees; selling his car; going through his personal effects; and closing out the apartment. All of it needed to be done in one week's time.

By the time I drug myself step-by-step up the ramp leading to the funeral home's entrance, I was completely alone, and the strain was setting in. I was fully aware that lots of decisions still needed to be made in the days ahead, but I didn't want to make them. Everything in me wanted to run the opposite direction. But I had no choice. This task was mine alone, and I was not going to let my grandfather down. Someway, somehow, I managed to open the doors and walk through them holding two suit options. Not until after the burial would I realize that I had completely forgotten to bring ties.

"My grandfather would have died if he'd known he was buried without a tie!" I wailed to a relative over the phone.

"Stephanie," she consoled, "He is already dead. He'll never know."

That may have been true, but I felt devastated. That man wore ties with his suits! I do think, however, that I got one choice right. I had to decide whether or not to bury my grandfather with his wedding ring. That was a tough one; but, once I considered my grandparents' seventy-year love story, I knew what I had to do. The ring went with him.

The morning of the funeral, I headed to the nearest Starbucks for a much needed apple fritter and coffee. The gravesite was two hours from Gramps' apartment, so I had quite a drive ahead of me. When I pulled up to the pay window, my cell phone buzzed. I gulped to see that it was a call from work.

"Stephanie," an irritated voice greeted my ear, "were you going to call in for this conference call or were we to call you?"

In the craziness I had completely forgotten offering to help with a volunteer training project at my company. "Well …" I searched for words. "I am on my way to a funeral actually."

Surely, I thought, *they'll give me a pass. It's just a brainstorming meeting!*

"Well, are we ready to begin?" the leader said with an aggravated edge to her voice.

I took a deep breath and plunged into the call. In the long run, I was grateful for the distraction. In three hours, I would deliver my grandfather's eulogy. I certainly needed to practice in the car, but I had cried so much up to that point that I welcomed a mental break.

When the phone meeting ended, my friend from Santa Barbara called and let me try to practice the service as I drove. Words barely came out as tears and sobs flowed. That friend was and is still such a gift. I marveled at her strength and patience with me.

When I arrived at the funeral home, I was ushered into the room where my grandfather's body and casket waited for my personal "viewing." Since it was just going to be Gramps and me during this special time, I couldn't hold back.

"You've got a lot of nerve, Huffman—leaving me like this." I mumbled through a crooked smile.

At that point the small debate began. "Should I? Shouldn't I?" Suddenly, my hand shot out. As I touched Gramp's fingers, which felt like cool wood, a strange comfort came over me. His body might lay in front of me, but his spirit danced in a much better place far, far away.

YOU'RE KIDDIN' ME, RIGHT?

"Hey," the funeral director's voice broke into my thoughts. "There's a friend of mine that wants to meet you. I have told him all about you. He was a test pilot at the nearby base and would like to take you out tonight. His name is Fuzzy."

The director had been absolutely wonderful to me during the entire ordeal, but I could not believe she suggested I agree to a blind date. I wondered if I'd entered the Twilight Zone, or was an unsuspecting victim of some new, bizarre version of *Candid Camera* or *Punked*.

Gathering all of the composure I could muster, I stammered for a moment and tried to determine just exactly how to answer.

"Well," I paused, "Uh, you know, I think, I uh, would just cry through the entire date. You know, I am burying my Grandfather in a few minutes, and I'm afraid I might just boo hoo through the whole thing. But um, you know, maybe uh coffee? I, uh, have to head back tonight, but I could squeeze him in at say, oh, 2pm?"

I reached for the nearest Kleenex box.

Accepting a blind date during my Grandfather's viewing? Do people really do that?

I was either incredibly desperate, weakened by my current emotional state or simply amused. The fact that my Grandfather was still looking out for me, or perhaps was playing a delightful prank only made me laugh. He had worked at that base and knew a lot of test pilots. Perhaps, even in his departure, he was trying to set me up. But the blind date didn't quite pan out.

I never did meet Fuzzy. Guess he figured that asking a girl out on the day she laid her grandfather to rest might not be the classiest of moves.

MISSION ACCOMPLISHED

Throughout that week, I managed to work through all of my grandfather's personal effects. A delightful family I've known for years came and spent the entire day helping me sort, toss, and clean. They made a very difficult task not only bearable but enjoyable. They were my angels.

With the apartment cleaned out, I had five days left to sell the car. It wasn't until I relinquished the keys to its new owner that I learned it was illegal to post a for "sale sign" in a car's window. I'd been all over Southern California's freeways, but I wasn't pulled over once. Breathing a prayer of thanks, I boarded the plane back to Texas. I was more than relieved. I felt victorious. I'd only been in California seven days, but I'd accomplished my mission in its entirety. Finally, I could relax and refocus on something that had patiently awaited my full attention: my job.

Security at the airport had another agenda. Apparently, a tiny pocket-knife of my granddad's made it into one of my carry-ons. In one bag, I carried his American Indian jewelry collection (stones that weighed about thirty-five pounds in all). In the other bag were personal items that I wanted to protect. As they ripped open compartments, dumped them upside down, and scattered Gramps' belongings onto the table, I not only got mad—I cried.

Security wasn't fazed by my tears. They forced me out of line and escorted me back to the check-in counter as if I were a threat. There I was ordered to check one of the bags that carried my precious belongings. *This isn't good*, I thought, *It'll never make it to Texas*. The television specials I'd seen about greedy bag handlers replayed through my mind.

"That will be one hundred dollars," the clerk announced flatly "to check this extra bag."

PHOENIX ISN'T THE ONLY THING THAT'S HOT

Shuffling down the aisle in search of my seat, I had a sudden thought and froze midstride. One of the security personnel had placed the envelope holding the cash from the car sale into the wrong carry on. Although I had repeatedly asked him to be careful and had tried to watch, he had shoved that envelope into the very bag I was forced to check at the last minute.

Sinking into my seat, I literally could not see or hear the world around me. My mind screamed, *Some airport employee will get the money I needed to cover the funeral and my travel expenses!*

I stared at the tray table in front of me and wanted to crawl under that floating seat cushion they always tell you about. I felt frustrated, physically ill, and painfully fatigued.

"Did the pilot just say it's 128 degrees in Pheonix?" the male passenger to my left asked, his voice buzzing into my conscience like an unwanted fly.

Dazed, I looked in the direction of the window and tried to make my eyes focus. Couldn't this guy see I was in extreme emotional distress? Besides, I knew I looked like a wreck. Why on earth would anyone strike up a conversation with a washed up, middle-seat passenger who was apparently ready to pass out?

I prepared my retort for this would-be, conversant seatmate, but when I really looked at him, I stopped. The guy was drop-dead gorgeous and had every intention of carrying on a conversation with me. His eyes not only eased the pain of the last thirty minutes in flight but could have erased my memory of the last thirty years!

This prized, Latin specimen explained he was an Executive Chef, and finally asked for my card which I already had waiting in my hands! Though he walked with me to my terminal before we parted ways, I haven't heard from him since. But he sure was a visual and mental vacation for a few sweet moments!

Feeling quite girly after our encounter, and oh-so-much better, I headed to my gate for the connecting flight. But my plane wasn't there to meet me; Murphy's Law had pulled up instead. I was informed that the flight had been cancelled, and no flights were available for the next three days! Ironically, that bad news was just the miracle I needed. For some reason, the airlines demanded that passengers go to baggage claim, reclaim their luggage, re-check in, and then re-check bags while going through security all over again. This meant I'd have a chance to retrieve the bag holding the cash from the car sale! If God was in His heaven, and if the stars would just align, that money would be waiting for me when I reached the carousel.

Upon spotting my bags, I frantically dropped everything, then reached for, and ripped open the satchel. There, to my utter disbelief, was the cool, green cash. A cry of elation rose from the bottom of my toes and exited through my mouth. God not only provided a beautiful man to relieve my trauma, but He allowed the cancellation of my connecting flight so that I could get my bag and reclaim the money I needed. Life was good; but I was still physically, emotionally, mentally, and spiritually depleted. All I wanted was my mom and my dog.

When I finally arrived back in Texas at 3:00 a.m. in the morning, I looked forward to assisting my family with the celebration of my grandmother's ninetieth birthday. But all too soon, I had to pack, yet again, for a crucial round of presentations. This time I was headed to New York.

While sitting in the salon chair to await the flight, my hands started to itch. By the time I landed in the Big Apple—after missing my original flight due to morning traffic—the itching had graduated to full blown chest pains and hives that produced deep, red welts all over my body. But since a single girl's gotta work, I trudged on. Though I literally had no ability to think past the moment, people depended on me. Projects awaited my attention. And so the beat went on.

Before me lay a business trip to Orlando and my biggest and best week of the year. Ten to thirteen presentations would be given by me once I landed, but I loved this part of my life. I looked forward to meeting with the people I was going to connect with at the upcoming event. That bit of positive energy kept my engine running though my body and mind ran on empty.

As I looked out the window of the plane, I took a moment to breathe and reflect. Sure, I had grown up knowing that I would one day care for my mother and my grandparents in their final days. I also had known that I would need a job conducive to picking up and going when the time came. But what overwhelmed me the most, as (in my mind) I relived those last few weeks, was the surprise gift of my very fabulous, and very concerned, friends back in Nashville. They had cared for and supported me during the entire ordeal through e-mails, texts, and check-in visits to my house. My circle of friends helped me navigate my very stormy seas.

Most single gals never receive life's call to care for the elderly alone while trying to juggle an active career. But for those who will face situations similar to these, I say, "If I survived and lived to tell, so will you."

We're a tough lot, we singles. I've seen more than a few of us take out the blender and the sugar when life called to say, "The lemons have arrived, and they're at the front door!"

Chix Chat:

1. If you will one day be responsible for the care of individuals in your life, list their names.
2. Summarize discussions you've had with them regarding their future care.
3. Do you have a financial advisor with whom you can discuss this responsibility? If not, set up an appointment to do that or place a call of inquiry.
4. Do you have access to the accounts of the person you will care for someday? If not, learn how they plan for you to handle their finances and personal matters when they are unable to do it for themselves.
5. Has the individual you will care for discussed their preferences for funeral arrangements such as where they plan to be buried? If so, write them down. If not, plan to have the discussion soon.
6. If you've not addressed your possible responsibilities in caring for this person with your family, your friends, and your boss, make plans to do so soon. Enlisting support now and knowing who will care for you as you care for others can prove a big help in the future.

Chapter 11

A Divine Holiday

"Accept the place the divine providence has found for you, the society of your contemporaries, the connection of events."
— *Ralph Waldo Emerson*

EVER noticed that life rarely hands you one stressful event at a time? I've found that, about the second I think I've recovered from one difficulty, another takes its place. Shortly after my grandfather's passing, during that final business trip, I sensed in my spirit that something wasn't quite right.

Word was out at the convention that reorganization was coming, and we all knew what that really meant. Layoffs. Deep down, I had that gnawing feeling. Over the years, I'd watched as friends and associates were let go from their jobs. This time I couldn't help but think that my number had finally come up. Major changes within the business had started at the beginning of the year. Odd interactions and interchanges had occurred for months. A few coworkers started acting strangely. *Besides,* I mentally sighed, *it seems to fit the way the summer has been going, so why not add a layoff to the fun?*

Twenty-four hours after returning from Orlando, I began to follow up with business contacts I had made during that week. When an e-mail from my boss suddenly blinked into the in-box, I gulped.

"When did you say you'd be back in the office?" he questioned.

I knew by the sound of his voice that something wasn't right. I quickly dialed the office, but he and his assistant were no longer taking calls. It was only 3:00 p.m. on Friday afternoon, and Monday seemed like an eternity away. In desperation, I text-messaged my boss: "If you had to lay me off, I understand. Just please, let me know."

His answer came swiftly: "I'm sorry. There's no easy way to do this. We'll talk Monday."

Sure enough, in spite of all I'd done to juggle all the plates spinning in my life, I got laid off. The company for which I had so diligently and loyally worked, more than fifteen years, simply did away with, and outsourced, my job.

As I sat in Panera Bread, my new office of choice at my Texas home base, I tried to wrap up all the loose ends. I was still stunned that I was sans salary, but I kept trudging forward hoping to make for a smooth transition back at headquarters.

Thankfully, a much-anticipated beach trip with my girlfriends was just around the corner. I knew, if I could just make it a few more days, I would be able to escape my rough summer and re-energize for the coming job hunt that would mark a new chapter in my life.

Knowing that time at the coast was coming in July had kept me going as the tears streamed down in my grandfather's apartment back in June. The thought of that get-a-way had assured me that there would, one day, be time and room to cry as I spoke the eulogy over his grave. Knowing I would soon hear waves crashing on the shore soothed me as the hives threatened to drive me over the edge on the plane ride to New York. So when I finally jumped in the car with the girls for our Florida retreat, I was ready for the much-anticipated respite. But the tension didn't ease.

WELL, BLOW ME OVER!

In the middle of our vacation, however, a phone message came in from my neighbor: "Stephanie. Well, ya' see, there's been a storm ... I don't know how to tell you this, but a tree fell on your roof."

My stomach sank.

A few calls and some wacky converstations later, I learned that, indeed, a tree had fallen on my roof. I spent the remaining days of our time away on the phone, working with contractors and my insurance company to put my house back into order. I couldn't see the damage, but helpful friends back home kindly took photos and sent them to me via e-mail.

Oddly, I never panicked—at least not completely—over the tree situation. With friends like the ones I had, I truly had little to worry about. As I recalled the incredible ways God had handled so many thousands of details and needs over the previous weeks, it didn't seem prudent to doubt His assistance in the latest situation.

As if to verify the point, a contractor informed me that the tree had fallen on the perfect corner of the house. Squirrels had taken up residence in my attic and, unbeknownst to me, had created a huge nest. The resulting hole from the felled tree exposed their handiwork. With one swish, the nest was gone. It was the size of a large ottoman, and removing the roof was the only way to get it out. That tree, however, did the trick.

The girls at the beach house were a big help in keeping my mood light during those difficult days. One of them began referring to me as "Shipwreck," while other girls back home dubbed me "Job-etta" (a feminine play on Job, an Old Testament man who underwent immense trials and pain). The girls' well-meaning jibes kept me laughing. But my favorite line of the summer came not from my beach buddies but from a friend back at home.

As I wearily sat on the steps of our cottage in the rain, I dialed that friend's number with the plan to appeal for assistance. I knew the tree had not only smashed my air conditioning unit, but it had managed to tear the electric meter completely from the wall of the house, too. Apparently, all of the cords, wires, and cables were exposed; and the national weather service reported rain, thunder, and lightening back in Nashville. I needed to get someone over there to flip the breakers—quickly.

"Um," I said into the phone, wishing my friend had picked up so I wouldn't need to leave an awkward message, "I know that you might be passing by my house on your way home tonight. Uh, when you get this, could you call me? I, uh, was wondering if you could drop by my place for a few minutes. You see, apparently, well, there's a tree on my roof."

Moments later, my friend's name lit up my cell phone. Knowing she had just heard my message, I clicked the answer button. I heard her say in a dead pan tone, "Well, of course there is a tree on your house."

We both laughed aloud at her observation of the state of my life. Gramps was gone. My job deleted. My home a mess. In one sentence she managed to perfectly sum up my entire summer, which was turning out like a really bad made-for-TV-movie. (One for which I was desperately waiting for the final credits to roll.)

My friend not only stopped by and turned off the breaker box, but she also personally called a contractor who handled the tree removal and covered the immediate needs in the house. That night another friend headed over with flashlights and ice chests. She, along with her roommate, emptied my refrigerator and took all salvageable items to another home. I was amazed at how my friends stepped in and took control and were determined to take care of *me*.

That autumn brought a few more unwelcomed surprises—like the squirrels in my teacups and the ones I found mating on the chair in my home office. (Yes. You read that correctly.) But I handled each upset pretty well. Not because I was so amazingly strong or courageous, but because people were assisting me, loving me, praying for me, and proving to me that friends are a most precious commodity.

My friends were the island ahead of me. They were also the little life preservers that kept my head above water during my journey to the shore. I was overwhelmed by their care, their thoughtfulness, their attention to detail, their selflessness, and their concern. I could go on for days about them. I always thank the Lord for giving them to me.

> *Friends are a precious commodity.*

My trip to the shore was a holiday I had planned and looked forward to enjoying. The surprise lay off was an imposed holiday that God had allowed, if not orchestrated, on my behalf. I look back at the situation as a divinely inspired holiday. Without that wild week, I might never have experienced the fact that the people in my life will quickly come to my rescue in the midst of life's storms.

That's a truth I'll always hold dear.

Chix Chat:

1. What practical steps can you take should a life-changing event such as a lay-off come your way? If you have a current savings plan in place for emergencies, describe it.
2. Do you take a brief holiday or break when life gets tough? Explain your answer.
3. Consider which of your friends and family members have keys to your home. Whom should you notify when going out of town?
4. Choose an emergency contact or two and invite those people over, showing them where to find the circuit breaker, water main, and other important details of your home.
5. Collect the numbers of your pest control specialist, veterinarian, landlord, and anyone else who might be needed in handling an unexpected situation. Be sure to place or update their numbers in your cell phone or PDA.

CHAPTER 12

Lay Offs, Life Changes, and Other Scary Stories

"A cord of three strands is not quickly torn apart."
—*Ecclesiastes 4:12, NASB*

IT'S one thing to have great friends who take good care of us during our crazy times. It's another thing to return their favors, and I truly wanted to do that for the girls who saw me through my grandfather's passing and my layoff. Little did I know, my chance would come much sooner than I imagined.

In the early months of 2008, my friends and I didn't realize that the layoffs we saw in our area were just the beginning of an international crisis. In my city alone, over two hundred people within my industry were laid off within a six-month period. People I knew in other industries were also losing their jobs at a rapid pace. Every day the news announced more and more job losses. Watching the five o' clock report became increasingly overwhelming and frightening.

As I attended networking sessions and other career building opportunities, I entered rooms packed full of the fellow unemployed. Most of them were asked to leave nice jobs with substantial paychecks. My heart broke for those who had families. But I did wonder if people who looked at this single gal really understood my dilemma. For many of us single gals, there is *no* one to fall back on when employment ends. No partner to share in paying the mortgage, or the car payment, or the insurance, or the grocery bill, or the utilities while we get back on our feet.

While girlfriends can't necessarily help one another out financially, they can provide an important base of support during a crisis. My friends and I meet together for coffee, go on walks, chat by phone, and encourage each other online during our times of transition. We are there for each other every step of the way. Having one another's compassionate support means so much.

CHLOE'S TURN

On the last day of our beach house trip—the one that was supposed to be our vacation—Chloe received an e-mail from her manager. The wording was eerily familiar to one my manager left me the week prior. As we backed out of the driveway and headed off to dinner that night, Chloe reminded our traveling group of gals that her job had only existed a little over two years. She knew her company could live without it once again. My heart sank for her as our friends and I watched her privately processing, yet trying to remain calm and stay positive. When Chloe called her manager later that evening, she learned they'd deleted her position.

After that trip, Chloe and I—both unemployed—had a lot of free time, and more time for each other. Going for long walks seemed a great form of therapy for both of us.

"I cried myself to sleep for many nights after that call," Chloe admitted during one of our chats, "I'm a single woman. If I don't bring home the bacon, I don't eat. Add house payments and a troublesome car with over one-hundred-and-fifty-five-thousand miles on it, and you have some concerns."

Before her last day in the office, Chloe all but wrapped up a major upcoming project for the department, updated her resume, met with a career placement company, and started shopping for a computer; she stayed busy, and she remained positive. But all too soon, Chloe went from feeling appreciated and respected to recognizing that she, as an employee, was completely dispensable. Though she scoured internet sites, made phone calls, sent e-mails, and had coffee with everyone she could convince to meet with her, she soon felt the world passing her by. She had no role in it, no specific place to be, no one waiting on her or needing her to leave the four walls of her house. The universe was continuing on without her, whether or not she held a job.

One of the most trying things both of us faced during our seasons of layoff was the frustration of the constant questions of well-meaning friends and acquaintances. Found a job yet? Are you working? Do you have a severance package? Are you on unemployment?

"I wish people were better at handling a friend's layoff," Chloe said one day, "It really bothers me when people greet me by asking if I've found a job yet. A simple, 'Hi, how are you?' or 'How was your week?' would've be so much more encouraging!" Well said.

I've decided that the best way to help a friend handle a layoff, or any major crisis for that matter, is to wait and let them talk about the situation when they are ready. No one wants to continually admit, "No, I do not have a job," or "Yes, I know it's been months." Nobody needs constant reminders about a bad health report or a personal disaster. True friends let friends just talk about everyday life. They don't push for details.

In time, Chloe applied for a part-time retail job at a home décor store in the mall. With a Bachelor's degree in Business and over fifteen years in her previous industry, filling out multiple applications alongside seventeen-year old high school seniors was humbling. One moment she'd sat with a successful author discussing their next project; and the next, she found herself asking the twenty-year-old employee behind the cash register, "Are you hiring?"

I was so proud of her. The interior design thing was in her blood, and I knew she'd do great at a home decorating store. But going from a very nice paycheck to a meager hourly wage proved another challenge. Frustrating too were the days when people who were familiar with her career history, came in as store customers. Seeing her behind a cash register seemed to catch them off guard. Sometimes, she'd slip back to the stock room and hide, hoping they'd leave and she'd go undetected.

My friend is a woman of very strong faith, so I wasn't surprised to hear her explain that the days she chose to focus on her faith in Christ were altogether different from those when she focused on herself. Chloe realized that her worst days occurred when she chose to think about what she'd lost rather than the new possibilities the Lord was sending her way and orchestrating on her behalf.

> *The worst days occur when we choose to think about what we've lost instead of the new possibilities.*

A few months into the job, Chloe's store manager handed her some papers. He encouraged her to apply for an Assistant Buyer position in the corporate offices of the company. His confidence in her at that time was the very medicine this post-laid off employee needed. However, if she moved forward into the new world, she'd be entering an entirely different industry. Chloe applied but didn't really give it much thought. Weeks went by and no word. She even pursued other options while she waited, but nothing concrete ever developed.

A week or so before Christmas, Chloe received a call from company headquarters. Was she available for an interview? She interviewed three times in ten days and received an offer by New Year's Eve.

After much prayer and personal searching, Chloe accepted the offer and started her new job fifteen days after the first interview.

"God's timing was amazing," she said, "I never went a day without health insurance. The day one ended, was the day the next one went into effect!"

Months of waiting finally came to an end for my dear friend. Hers wasn't the path she would have chosen, but she admits that some of the most exciting times in her life came from the things not planned. Chloe has since shared that she learned a lot about God's sovereignty and His provision during her crisis, but she focuses most on the fact that she learned to realize just how much God loves her and is involved in every detail of her life. She faced layoff and survived—even landed in a more challenging place than when she started out. Life is good.

It's now been almost a year, and Chloe will tell you that changing careers at forty-one isn't for the faint of heart. She still feels awkward in her new adventure.

"I must say," she admitted one evening as we discussed her lay-off and new position, "that starting a new career makes you take stock of what defines you. If your identity is based on what you do or how you perform, then you're liable to have some scratches and dings in your self-image."

Overcoming difficulties is a daily journey. But when we allow our friends to walk beside us, we don't need to walk the path alone.

GIGI'S SURPRISE

Sometimes, life's surprises can be blessings in disguise. One friend admitted to praying that God get her out of the rut her life had become. A year later, after having endured massive personal upheaval, she jokingly warns me not to pray that one lightly.

Many of us tend to live in ruts. We settle for the familiar rather than pursuing our dreams or stretching ourselves. We need our worlds shaken up a little to move us further down the path that's right for us.

GiGi is in her forties and not-yet-married. When she pursued her Masters in graduate school, she had thoughts of working in the entertainment industry. After graduation, however, she took a safe, government job, upgraded from her parents' hand-me-down car, and bought a starter home. When the opportunity came to work at one of the largest entertainment agencies in the world, it meant leaving her parents, her friends, her house, and even her church behind to start over. But she did it. Less than five years and two promotions later, Gigi was finally able to do what she moved five hundred miles away to accomplish.

Nine years into Gigi's dream job, she walked into a board room and heard the words she never expected to hear: "We have decided not to renew your contract."

While they blamed the economic downturn, Gigi knew the reason didn't matter. She had no job, no husband's income to fall back on, no parents to run home to, and no insurance. Though she had the foresight to live outside of debt, she felt her options were limited and her time short.

Gigi decided she never wanted to live at someone else's disposal again—recession or not. If she were to invest ten hours of herself a day, she wanted to make it count. After some much needed rest, time to think and pray, Gigi launched her own artist management company. A new journey began.

> *We settle for the familiar rather than pursuing our dreams.*

When I look back at the sudden changes and events life brought to not only me, but Chloe and Gigi, I can't imagine our lives turning out any differently. The new worlds that opened to us as a result of our lay-offs have been challenging, but they have brought new friends and adventures we never would have had the chance to enjoy without them.

I've come to understand that fighting change and upheaval in my life can be detrimental. By doing so, I miss out on what Providence may be trying to bring my way. Only by embracing life and what it brings do we truly experience life to the fullest.

"I HAVE WHAT …?"

One friend's story made my bout with job loss seem less jarring, and it reminded me that many situations require us to reevaluate life and approach it with a renewed sense of purpose.

I hadn't seen Dottie for quite some time; so when we caught up at a professional event, I expected that lunch with her would be full of frivolity and fun.

Dottie is over fifty and she—like Chloe, Gigi, and me—has never married. A talented video producer, she's also a gifted writer and has always been able to make me laugh. Over time, we'd lost touch. So you can imagine my surprise when I heard her latest news.

"I've had cancer," she reported. "Had it for two weeks. Surgery got it all."

I was truly horrified. And embarrassed that I hadn't even known or been aware that she was ill. But as her story began to unfold, I found myself deeply saddened for my friend. It was the part about her surgery and the decision to have all of her female organs removed that hurt me the most.

"I used to joke that I'd *pay* to have someone take out my uterus," she said in her humorous, deadpan way, "But when the time came, I wasn't so sure. I asked my sister, 'What if I decide I want kids?!'"

We both laughed, but we also knew that the topic wasn't funny. For the most part, the single women I know or have met always dreamed that they would one day grow up, get married, and have children. This dear friend would never experience the latter. It was a life change she would have to accept. And it was permanent.

IT'S ALL GOOD

Driving back to my office, I tried to process what all this upheaval I was experiencing and learning about from others could mean. First I got laid off, then Chloe did, then Gigi did, and then Dottie had to say goodbye to a dream. If that wasn't enough, another single friend had to leave her dream job overseas to care full-time for her aging and ailing parents in the states.

"We're more adaptable and capable than you'd think," I found myself saying out loud, "We're strong. And we have each other. That's what we've got to get out of all this."

As if on cue, the song from the 1970s hit *The Mary Tyler Moore Show* started playing in my mind, *"We're gonna make it after all ... "*

These days my friends and I navigate our "new normals." During those months of walks, coffee meetings, phone calls, and lunches, we gradually came to understand that yes, we will make it, though sometimes we'll need a little extra help and some added direction.

In the following chapters, I'll share three tools I created during my time of transition to keep me paddling in the *right* direction. I hope they'll do the same for you.

Chix Chat:

1. What practical steps have you researched or considered taking in order to prepare for a life-changing event such as a lay-off?
2. Do you have a "rainy day" plan to help you when a life crisis strikes? If so, what is it? If not, begin creating one today. You may find that getting together with a friend and asking her to share hers proves helpful. Her ideas may get you started.
3. Which of your friends are currently experiencing life crises? Set up time to join each of them for coffee or a meal. Find practical ways to assist them in what they're facing; maybe offer to care for their homes while they are away or to run errands to help out.
4. Who in your circle might be willing to join you in meeting the needs of a friend experiencing a life crisis? Give that friend a call and formulate a helping plan.
5. Consider who has experienced and survived a life crisis similar to one your friend is enduring. With your friend's permission, invite that person to join you both for dinner so that she can share some wisdom on the subject and provide hope and encouragement.

Part 4

Goals & Dreams

CHAPTER 13

Out of the Darkness and Into the Light

> *"There is in every true woman's heart a spark of heavenly fire, which lies dormant in the broad daylight of prosperity; but which kindles up, and beams and blazes in the dark hour of adversity."*
> —Washington Irving

IF you've ever experienced a sudden crises or dramatic life change, you know that universal feeling that often accompanies one. It's as if you sit on a carousel that keeps spinning faster and faster though no one manages the controls. Just when you try to get off, you realize that holding on for dear life and riding it out is the safest option. Sometimes, the effort is so exhausting that you merely pray for it to stop. Deep down, though, you know the moment will come when you simply have to jump off and face the risk.

When I finally found a moment to breathe after my grandfather's passing and the stress of the layoff, I got myself together and leapt off the ride I'd endured for months. I knew it was time to break away from the chaos that dominated my summer, to get back on my feet, and to find a way to make my new normal work.

Slowly I came to realize that life was never going to be the same. There would be no more trips out to California to visit Gramps and no more trips to Manhattan to visit clients. There was no going back. But to be honest, I was okay with that. In a way, I was relieved.

I had long needed a break, and suddenly I faced one. The fact that I had been laid off was not so much a problem as a taste of early retirement. I loved my new found freedom and the opportunity to rest, think, and relax. Having grown so exhausted over the summer, it was a treat to sit at home with no set schedule or agenda. I had goals and dreams, and I could only imagine that this was the opportune time to give them some thought.

I knew I needed to come up with a plan to get me moving forward once again. I wasn't sure how I would accomplish that, and I didn't have a clue as to where or how to begin. I did know, however, that I couldn't sit on the couch and drink coffee forever.

My grandmother always encourages me to make lists when facing a major decision or a tough job. "Write things down," she says. "Get it on paper, and then take it from there." My grandmother has kept yellow legal pads and post-it notes and lists all over her house for as long as I can remember. Her wisdom showed me where I needed to start. I sat down and got out my favorite pad and pen. With those in hand, my list—as well as my renewed sense of direction—began to take shape.

I began by collecting positive sayings, powerful quotes, and pithy comments I had read or heard that spoke happy truths into my life. Here are a few favorites:

> *"Just be sure that every step you take is headed in the right direction."*
> *- Unknown*

> *"The very worst waste of time is doing something very well that need not be done at all."-Unknown*

> *"Care about people's approval and you will be their prisoner."*
> *- Tao Te Ching*

I planned to keep these and many others like them handy for review every morning. I also decided to take to heart the life approach of one particular woman from whom I'd received an e-mail. I asked her to meet with me to discuss a business opportunity I was considering, but she made it clear that, unless I were interested in her multi-level marketing plan, she would not have time to meet with me. Why? She was successful and very busy. She hoped I'd understand. Our honest interchange forced me to take a good look at just where my time, energy, and resources were truly going. That woman was focused and disciplined; surely,

I could learn from her. I started looking for ways to incorporate her sense of focus to my situation.

I began by making a list of the people in my life who receive my time during a week. It included those whom I e-mailed, those whom I called daily and weekly, and a host of folks I count as true friends. After that, I noted the places I go. That showed where I spent my time online and my time with friends or away from the house. It also revealed how much of my life belonged to organizations where I volunteered. Soon I gained a better understanding of who and what took up the precious hours of my day—and not my week.

These lists led me to ponder deeper questions: *Where am I going? What am I really trying to accomplish?* Their answers led to more self-evaluation: *How can I plan to get where I want to go? Why do I want to achieve that in the first place?* Soon I was able to lay out my inner hopes, goals, passions, and dreams. I started to see the value of focusing on me. I realized that doing so was neither selfish, nor inappropriate, nor rude; instead, it was a necessary part of helping me move beyond my current status.

I needed to do something. I needed renewed energy for life. But I'd not find it without some much needed assessment and readjustment.

We girls need to routinely evaluate what we do on a daily and weekly basis. That's why you should consider who and what in your life can get you closer to attaining your goals, hopes, and dreams. You may find that some of the people and activities receiving your time hold you back. You might need to reevaluate your relationships and the way you spend afternoons and evenings.

When a single gal gets home from work, her day truly begins. That's because whole piles of work are still waiting when we walk through the door. Dishes, laundry, bills, and more await our attention. But many times we find ourselves defaulting to long phone conversations or dinner out with a friend in order to debrief from a long or very rough day, and we also give away many precious hours to friends who need a shoulder to cry on. Many times, precious hours fly by and then we find ourselves only more behind and more frustrated. Striving to meet emotional needs as well as the daily, physical ones is a difficult balance. That's why we have to be careful about how we spend our time.

I found, after making my lists, that I was better able to determine what I truly longed for deep down inside. I got a better sense of who I was and where I would like to go. I found myself more determined to pour energy into those people who mean the most to me. Became more focused on withholding my time and energy from those organizations, people, and functions that might hold me back from achieving my heart's desires.

Eventually, my lists morphed into a grid. As time drew on, I noticed this new way of looking at my life on paper was not just revealing. It has become a living, working document of guidance. Tweaking it daily, if not weekly, helps me prioritize and motivate myself in this new stage of life.

As I mentioned in the last chapter, many of my friends have experienced recent changes, personal losses, the death of a loved one, the unexpected end to important relationships, and the loss of a job. They completely understand that chilling, "What do I do now?" or "Where do I even begin?" feeling that can wrap around us like a fog and make life seem overwhelming.

My friend Lynn called to talk through the pros and cons of taking on a part-time job. The longer she talked, the more concerned I became. Lynn already held a pretty demanding full-time job and often seemed frazzled. I couldn't imagine how she'd squeeze anything else onto her to-do list.

"I'm in debt, Stephanie," she confessed, when I pressed her to explain why she wanted the job in the first place. "I am determined to get out."

"You know you're an over-achiever, right?" I chided.

"Yes, I do," came the whiny reply. It was then I wondered if the exercise I was creating for myself would be of help to her.

I encouraged her to grab a piece of paper and mark off four separate sections like this:

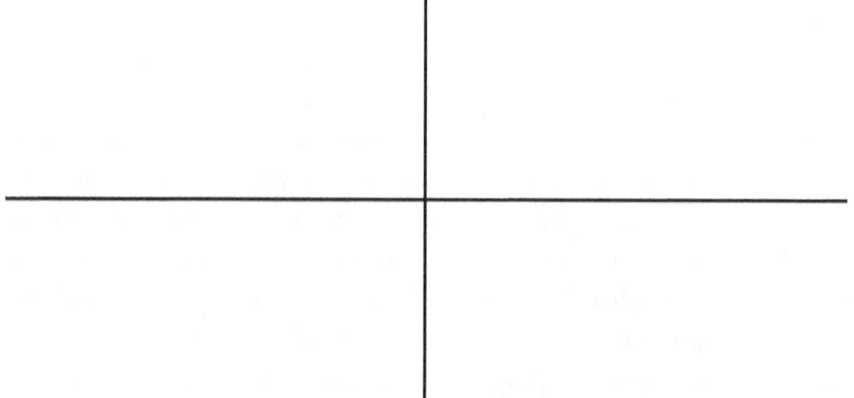

"Who, on any given day, gets your time, your energy, and your resources?" I asked.

"In that upper right square, I want you to list who you call, who you e-mail, who you chat with at work, and who you lunch and carpool with."

"Uh, huh," she mumbled distractedly as she scribbled her responses.

"Now, beneath that," I encouraged, "I want you to list all the places you go. Where do you give your time, your energy, your resources? You can put things like organizations, the office, time you spend at the book store, the gym, whatever."

"Um," she hesitated after a few moments, "I'm running out of space! Do I need to include the time I spend on facebook or other online sites, too?"

"Yes," I insisted, "and don't forget to write down your study groups, social gatherings, volunteer projects, and your French class. Squeeze them in the box, Lynn. That's part of the point."

A few moments later, I asked my friend to write down her passions. Her vision.

"What do you really want in life?" I questioned. "Where would you really like to get involved? What do you really want to be doing?"

"Well," she said as she wrote, "I'd love to go on a trip to Italy! And I've been thinking about writing a column for a magazine. Of course, that might help me pay off my credit card and save a little money—those are high on my list of things to do! And I want to lose ten pounds. And I would love to ... "

"Good," I chuckled at her enthusiasm.

"Now, how about the board of the professional women's organization you and I both serve on? I didn't even hear you mention that."

"No," she replied after a moment's hesitation, "the truth is that I don't enjoy it much. It was just something to help me network, you know?"

"That's something for you to think about," I inserted. "You might want to consider working toward giving it up."

"I never thought about it that way," she said, voice brightening.

"Well, in that last box, I want you to list the people who are either in your life, could be in your life, or should be in your life who could help you make those goals come true. How can you align yourself with people who can help make your passions a reality?"

What followed was an eye-opening discussion. Surprisingly, few, if any of the people with whom she regularly spent time were directly connected to her dreams. The people whom she needed in her life to accomplish her visions for the future simply weren't there. Instead, everyone else and every possible meaningless activity received her time.

"I guess I need to make some adjustments," she admitted. "I need to make time in my schedule for the people and activities I *need*."

The next time I saw Lynn, she had taken the notes from our chat and had polished them into a very neat and tidy set of squares that would become the official grid exercise. What we had haphazardly worked through by phone was replaced with a meticulously drawn diagram that carried true purpose. It was beautifully done. And I could tell she had really spent some time on it.

The following evening, Lynn and I were at a board meeting for the women's organization of which we were members. I was the chairman at the time and wanted to take my board members through the same liberating exercise Lynn and I had so enjoyed. When I asked the team to go through the process, Lynn interjected and expounded on the virtues of what she called The Grid. She was pleased to report that, twenty-four hours since working through it over the phone, she had cancelled her Netflix™ membership and made several other adjustments that better helped her begin to evaluate what her goals, dreams, and passions really were. She'd also found ways to delete a few expenses (like club dues) that eliminated the need for a part-time job! (She did go ahead with the part-time job, but tendered her resignation as she realized it wasn't the best use of her time and energy.)

"Before, I just wasn't getting closer to my goals," she confidently reported. "Now, I see how my time and resources can best be spent elsewhere. I now know where."

By encouraging just a bit of self-examination, The Grid gave Lynn permission to say "no" to things that directed her energy to anyone and everything but her true passions, visions, and goals. It showed her that the power to change rested in her hands.

The key to moving past a point of chaos and into a successful future is to align yourself with the people and situations that can assist you with achieving your goals. If individuals and activities are not in your grid, you may need to make some adjustments.

> *The power to change rested in her hands.*

It's not selfish to align with people that might benefit your dreams. If you have God-given talents that are not being used, re-think the way you do life. If the desires of your heart are healthy, pure, and not harmful to others, there's nothing wrong with finding people and connections to assist you in making them a reality.

No matter what you are facing—a promotion, a move, a business venture, another boring weekend, or a shocking life-change—The Grid will help you find your way towards the light at the end of the tunnel. It will help direct you in the path you need to take. We'll go through all four quadrants of the exercise together and get you heading in the right direction—the direction of your heart!

Chix Chat:

1. What do you do when you feel stuck and are not moving forward?
2. What motivates you when you feel down or frustrated?
3. How do you find direction for your life?
4. Who or what drains you of energy?
5. Who or what asks a lot of you but rarely gives back or encourages you?
6. What talent or interest do you wish you were able to use more or further explore?

CHAPTER 14

Charting Your Course to Success

"Far and away the best prize that life offers is the chance to work hard at work worth doing."
— *Theodore Roosevelt*

THE girls and I use The Grid to help us determine how best to spend our time. A running joke among my circle of friends sounds like this: "Sorry! You're just not in my grid!"

Recently, I called one of the gals to join me for a movie. She giddily replied, "Thanks, Stephanie, but going to the theatre is not in my grid. I told you I am going back to school. I have a test tomorrow, and I have to study!"

Though I missed her at the movie, I was very proud of her. I wasn't the least offended by her determination to keep her priorities straight. I respected that. I want so much for her to be successful in all she does. I desire the same for you.

In the rough draft stage of this book, I asked some single gals to read through it and provide feedback. Repeatedly, I heard, "Stephanie, you need to put The Grid in this book. It helped us. Maybe it will help the readers, too." So here it is.

For time's sake, you're more than welcome to skip ahead a few pages and bypass these exercises; but I hope you'll work through these tools. The girls and I find them useful and enlightening.

A WALK THROUGH THE GRID

On a standard-sized piece of paper, draw a line down the middle from top to bottom. Bisect it in the center of the page from left to right. You will have four sections. Label them as follows:

The Keys to My Success	*People I Connect with Daily*
Dreams, Goals, Passions, and Visions	*Where I Go and What I Do*

UPPER RIGHT SIDE

In the upper right quadrant, list all of the people who regularly receive your time, your energy, and your resources. You can list your family members—both those you talk to daily and those with whom you keep in touch through intermittent e-mails or letters. Next, list your co-workers or teammates or business partners. Include various board members or organizational contacts with whom you regularly touch base. If you know you will e-mail, text, talk with on the phone, or see a person either daily or weekly, make sure he or she gets on the list.

> *Where and with whom are you investing?*

One girl who filled in the upper right side looked up with panic while creating her list and said, "Could I have another piece of paper? This quadrant has already taken the entire right side of my page!" Her life was so full of time-consuming relationships that she had no time for anything else.

WHY THIS QUADRANT IS IMPORTANT

I am amazed at how, some days, my energy level is really high, and other days it bottoms out. I'm discovering that I need to be increasingly strategic about where I invest my energy.

Every individual has needs and personality quirks that impact our lives as we interact with them. I have come to believe most friends fall into one of two categories: Tank Fillers and Energy Sappers. Some of the people in our lives energize us and send us on our way as better people. I call these individuals Tank Fillers. These are the folks with whom you want to spend time. When you're together, neither of you does all the talking. Instead, you're both engaged in the conversation, giving and receiving for mutual benefit. When you leave the presence of a Tank-Filler, you're usually the better for it.

Unfortunately, many interactions are spent with Energy Sappers. (And we all know who they are.) Sappers sneak into our schedules and drain us of precious time, energy, and resources—without the least bit of concern over our needs. They are so busy needing us to see them through every crisis that they seldom give thought to our feelings and responsibilities.

One person in my life would call and call until I picked up the phone. It didn't occur to her I was often at work on those occasions when she demanded my attention. She thought it a good idea for us to have a code—like "raining"—so that I'd know she *really* needed to talk and would, therefore, set everything else aside to talk with her when I received her voicemails or when she began a conversation with those words. While I understood that she was going through a very rough time, I couldn't feasibly meet her demands.

Filling a friend's emotional tank with encouragement and support in return is generally not the first thing on the mind of a Sapper. Sometimes, they are so wounded they simply don't have the capacity to consider others before themselves. That's why you and I have to be careful. We need to list and consider those people in our lives who find it easier to take than to give. If we spend more time with Energy Sappers than Tank Fillers, we better watch out.

I love to have company, and I have a lot of it. On one particular night, an out-of-town guest obviously needed to talk. I made it very clear to her before her arrival that I had an early morning appointment that required I get a good night's rest. In spite of that, we stayed up talking until 3:00 a.m. as I tried to be a good hostess.

There I sat, terribly tired. Yawning profusely. And in my pajamas. But my visitor never stopped talking. While I should have just interrupted and ended our evening, I didn't. I let that particular Energy Sapper steal my much needed opportunity to sleep.

Looking back, I realize I could have risen and said, "You know, as I mentioned before you came and several times throughout this evening, I have a very important appointment in the morning. I know it isn't best for you right now that we end our discussion. But I hope you will understand that it's very late, and it's best for me that I head to bed."

Somewhere along the way, we are taught that taking care of ourselves first is selfish. But there's a problem with applying that idea to every situation: sooner or later, we'll become doormats. My guest had no qualms about keeping me up to all hours even though I *needed* rest. She had her interests first and foremost, and she certainly felt no guilt about them. In allowing her to take over, I set myself up for failure at the recording studio the next morning. She could have said, "It's late. You have to get up. I know that. We can pick this up tomorrow. You go to bed." But she chose another path. Letting her do that cost me the energy and the resources I needed for success at the audio session.

Sometimes, what we might assume or feel is best for another person might not be best after all. At times, a gentle lesson in caring for others and setting boundaries may be best for both parties.

Understand, I'm not suggesting we spend time only with people who benefit us, or that we *always* put ourselves first. What I wish to express is this: we have only so much time and energy to give. They are precious commodities. Therefore, you and I need to be very careful in selecting who receives our resources.

If you have a commitment, a priority, or a task that needs your full attention, you have a right (and a duty) to stay focused. And while people in crises will inevitably come your way and you may feel the need to be there for them, you aren't the only person in their lives, and you won't have all the answers. I find it helpful to think about each situation in reverse. If a person calling on me has something they need to do, or if they personally are on the clock, they will generally let me know they are unavailable. They know their time is precious; it's up to me to let them know mine is, too.

These days, I know: 1) Not to pick up the phone or reply to a message while in the middle of another priority or deadline, and 2) I realize that I simply cannot play the role of God, or a therapist, for those who call on me at the drop of a hat. The needy people in my life need to understand that truth, too.

LOWER RIGHT SIDE

In the lower right quadrant, list the places you routinely go. Where do you spend your time, energy and resources? Include the gym, the office, the subway, your place of worship, the 501c3 where you volunteer, and the weekly meetings you attend outside of work. List practices and coaching sessions. Your morning coffee stop. Favorite stores where you shop for groceries and clothes. Also include Facebook, Twitter, other forms of media or websites where you "go" daily or weekly.

Many times, we don't realize exactly *where* some of our time, energy and finances are really going. This section exposes where you are currently investing those resources. Are the ones you see listed the most strategic in your life? Could you streamline any activities? Eliminate some and add others? Are the pennies and dollars you spend here or there being put to the best use? Only you will know, but the paper in front of you will often spell it out.

IN WHAT EXACTLY ARE YOU INVESTING?

Our twenty-four hour days in seven-day weeks are non-negotiable time frames. No matter how hard you try, you will not add more hours to your day; and you will never get more days in your week. Either you will manage them, or they will bury you.

One gal who filled out The Grid realized she was on Facebook four or more hours a day. I wondered: *How can this married woman, who works full-time, benefit from spending so much time online? How might she better use those hours?* I can't say that I was surprised when, a few months after our conversation, she had moved out of her family's home and was filing for divorce.

The entire right hand column is a personal report to you on *where* your precious hours and dollars are going. It can be very eye opening.

LOWER LEFT SIDE

The lower left side is my favorite part of The Grid. In that space, write down your passions, your visions, your goals, and your dreams. This is your personal box. The heart of who you are, who you should be, and who you can be. Do you want a new 401k or more mutual funds? Do you hope to become CEO of your favorite organization? Land that dream job? Obtain that overdue promotion? Lose ten pounds? Join that online dating service? Do you want more friends? Perhaps better quality friends? Want to visit Istanbul? Go ahead; write it down! It's safe here. No one gets to see this but you.

The lower left quadrant is critical. Whoever and whatever receives your time each day also takes your energy investment. If you compare what's in your lower left quadrant to what's in the other two spaces you've filled in, you'll quickly see whether the people and places in whom you invest are helping you toward your goals or holding them at bay. If, for instance, your neighbor or your co-worker is getting most of your time, then whatever you have placed in that lower left box will only get your leftovers. You may want to build stronger relationships with your girlfriends, but you may not have anything left to give them at the end of the week. The bottom line? Be sure you understand who and what should be receiving your best. Notice the discrepancies between your desires and your reality and then make those needed adjustments. Don't worry about what you need to change, think about what you can begin to adjust.

WHAT DO YOU REALLY WANT?

Sally had just finished filling out her lower left side and proudly announced that everything she listed connected to earning more money. Making money would solve her problems and allow her the freedom to do all the wonderful things that she wanted to do with her life. Not surprisingly, she invested much of herself in that endeavor. The problem was that this goal contradicted with another she failed to list: Sally wanted deeper friendships. She simply didn't have any time to make that happen.

I asked, "How do you intend to have fulfilling relationships when all of your goals are financial, Sally? If your time and energy are going to business ventures and networking every day, what time do you have to honestly invest in friends?"

> *Discover the discrepancies between desires and reality and then make needed adjustments.*

Sally was upset that she did not have close gal pals. People did not call her to go out or to spend time with them. What Sally didn't realize was that, when the people she supposedly wanted as friends saw her coming, they actually ran in the other direction. Why? Because every conversation she engaged in revolved around her businesses and how she'd like to ring them into it. She was unaware that she invested zero time and energy into anyone she knew unless the connection would profit her financially.

Reaching your goals comes down to a simple principle: If you don't feed and water a plant—it dies. If you don't feed and water your relationships or invest energy and effort into attaining your goals, you'll never build the friendships you desire, and you won't get where you want to go. You aren't born with friends. You cultivate them. Likewise, dreams rarely come true on their own. You've got to work toward them and make them happen.

UPPER LEFT SIDE

Welcome to your magic box. In the upper left side of The Grid, list the people who are either in your life, could be in your life, or should be in your life who could help you achieve your goals. Who do you know, or need to know, who can help you make those dreams come true? If you don't know them personally, who is able to introduce you to the people who may encourage your vision? These are the people with whom you need to align. Conscientiously investing your time, energy, and resources in the people on this new list will help you go for the gold.

Michael Phelps won eight gold medals in the Beijing Olympics because he previously aligned himself with individuals and opportunities that would get him to that goal. He pursued the coach, the team, and the locations that would help him succeed. In going for the gold, Michael had to find people who would encourage him in achieving his dream. He needed his family and their support, but he found that he had to leave his hometown and move to the place that had the best pool and training facilities. He also needed the best coach, so he went out and found a "gold-minded" one. Michael pursued friends and teammates who would partner with him in achieving his dream. Whatever was required to go for the gold, he made happen.

Can you imagine if Michael had not gone to the pool every day and only listened to his coach when he felt like it? Had that been the case, we'd never have seen that beautiful piece of history Michael made in China the summer of 2008.

If you want a new career or a more exciting tomorrow, but spend your day chatting with the same old friends and keeping the same routine, then you will continue down the path you now travel. Get busy making adjustments! If you're out of work, align yourself with the people and the places connected with, or involved in, the company or industry you wish to enter. If you want a friend who'll support you through it all, find someone who either understands or is familiar with your field of interest. Remember: aligning yourself with the right connections to your future requires that you strategically and correctly invest yourself as much as possible in the pursuit.

One friend desired financial peace and a secure retirement. Her mutual funds were losing money, and she needed to find someone or some organization that could help. She contacted a financial advisor and began making the time to check-in with him for guidance on where best to put her money. Soon her financial outlook dramatically improved.

Another girl I knew wanted to lose ten pounds, but she spent so much time with high-calorie intake friends that she needed to re-think who she went out with, where she went, and how often. Thankfully, she was able to add a new friend to her upper left side who has become a gym buddy. Today she's off and running. Literally!

A close friend wanted to purchase a home, but she had developed a monster habit of going out on the weekends and taking frequent trips and vacations. She was so upset to find herself still renting an apartment well into her forties. She had to consider making some adjustments. She realized that the job she held would never financially provide what she needed for home ownership. She's started pursuing a new one and has decided to take a break from her jet-setting lifestyle to start saving towards a down payment.

You might have to think hard about how to adjust and align yourself with people and institutions where upward mobility is a possibility for you. But be encouraged, and stick to it! Remember: your time, your energy and your resources are limited. How and where you invest yourself will determine how far you'll go. If you give your precious resources to everything and everyone except for what you see in your lower left quadrant, you can't be surprised or frustrated when your goals and dreams lie dormant.

I hope you'll adopt The Grid as a working document to aid in decision-making. Look at it daily. Make it your own. Acknowledge any adjustments that need to be made. Align yourself with the right people and invest in them.

Remember, every decision you make is an investment in your future. Decide wisely. And go for the gold!

Chix Chat:

1. As you filled in The Grid, which part most spoke to you?
2. What about your responses to it jumped out at you? Surprised you? Frustrated you?
3. Who or what takes more of your time, energy, and resources than you realized? Where or with whom would you prefer to invest yourself?
4. With whom will you align to help you reach one of your goals or dreams? If you don't already have a relationship with that person, who could introduce you to him or her?
5. What ideas for life did The Grid help generate?

CHAPTER 15

How Do You Eat An Elephant? (One bite at a time.)

> *"The vision must be followed by the venture. It is not enough to stare up the steps—We must step up the stairs."*
> —Vance Havner

IN the previous chapter, we walked through The Grid to gain a better sense of the value of relationships and the importance of spending our time wisely. I've not yet met anyone who felt completely confident with what a little self-revelation reveals. Most of us recognize our need to make adjustments to the way we do life. But making life changes can feel so overwhelming that you might be tempted to give up before really trying.

My friend Carrie instructed an exercise class I attended. I'd been observing her coming in habitually late for a few weeks and found that the signs of burn-out were more than apparent. Not only was she walking through the door after the official start time, but she was dressed in street clothes when she arrived and had to go change while we warmed ourselves up. It wasn't long before Carrie was calling me while I was driving to class, asking if I wouldn't mind setting up the room once I arrived. She assured me she was on her way and would be there soon. It didn't take a rocket scientist to determine that something wasn't right. So, one night I asked if she'd like to go for a chat.

As we sat at a small café table, I began sketching on a paper napkin that the fine establishment graciously provided. Carrie leaned in as I wrote while I wondered how many award-winning movies, as well as national laws, are plotted and scribbled on similar gratis papyrus.

I shared with Carrie a situation in which I'd recently found myself. A few years earlier, while holding down a full-time job. I'd been involved with a group of students at a small church. Not only had I become their leader and teacher, I had become their activities director and mentor as well. The commitment grew until I was spending a minimum of twenty or thirty hours a week in that venture. Soon, my social life and friends disappeared. Suddenly, the only people in my life were under the age of twenty-five, and my family rarely heard from me. That experience caused me to stop and take a good hard look at what I was doing with my life. I explained to Carrie that a little reflection helped me gain a new perspective that assisted in fixing the problem.

I handed Carrie the napkin across which I'd written the seven days of the week. I asked her to list, under each day's heading, exactly what she routinely did and where she went. A few moments before, I had asked Carrie if she was really enjoying the classes she was teaching. "I like the people," she sighed, "but the drive and my schedule are killing me." I knew she needed to pull back and take a good look at her week.

After a quick glance at me, Carrie began to fill-out my impromptu Weekly Assessment exercise. Her responses looked something like this:

Sunday	*Monday*	*Tuesday*	*Wednesday*	*Thursday*	*Friday*	*Saturday*
Go to church	teach classes					
Eat Lunch	Work at the mall					
Stay at friend's house until Evening Service	teach classes					
Evening Church Service	drive to orchestra practice					

While Carrie worked away, I began to scribble these words on a second napkin:

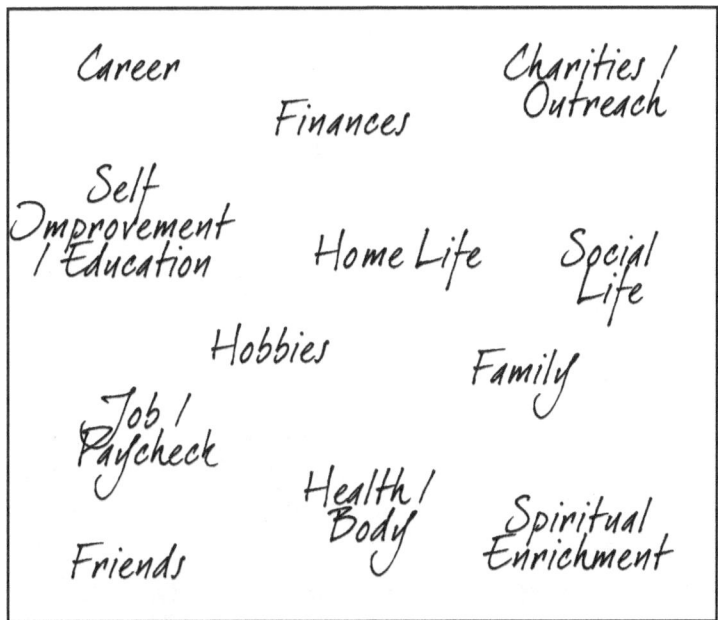

When my friend finished writing on her napkin, I handed her mine. I asked her to circle the words that represented where she saw most of her time going during a given week. I called these her Personal Investment Sectors. She glanced back at her Weekly Assessment paper, bit her lip, and slowly circled: Finances, Job, and Spiritual Enrichment. Her entire week went to the pursuit of those things! Little time or energy remained for anything else. Especially to her personal needs.

WHAT PERSONAL INVESTMENT SECTORS REVEAL

As most of us tend to do, Carrie gave the loudest and most urgent voices in her life control of her schedule. Surprisingly, those things didn't reflect her heart or meet her personal needs. Carrie was spending time working on a new career. But if truth be told, it wasn't a dream career. It was more of a job that helped pay off some debt. This venture was taking her to all ends of the county throughout the week. She was just saying "yes" to any and every opportunity that came her way.

The gas ate up any discretionary income, and the time she would have liked to spend with others was relegated to her commutes.

Carrie was spending a lot of time at her church, too. But sadly, this particular church was at the opposite end town; and, due to the distance, attendance was becoming more of an effort and an inconvenience than something to which she actually looked forward. Whereas Sunday can be a wonderful day of rest, Carrie was spending it everywhere but at home. Relaxing and preparing for Monday was no longer an option.

Carrie needed someone to help her stop the insanity and take a good look at what she was doing. She was no long in control of her schedule; it was driving her. Carrie needed some awareness of her out-of-kilter situation and some serious balance to even her out. That wouldn't happen without some strategic action on her part. My point in addressing this fact was not to discourage my friend; instead, I wanted to help her see that some of the things she would like to be doing were not circled. Everything she was doing, and everywhere she was going, was more of a "have to" than a "want to." Rather than shaping her life, she allowed it to just happen.

Carrie, literally, had zero time with any girlfriends each week, and she couldn't remember the last time she cleaned her home. She didn't know the last time she'd grocery shopped and found herself constantly eating on the go.

The realization seemed to waken something inside my friend. Streams ran down her cheeks, but they were happy tears. She looked as if the stress of the week were exiting her body. "How did you know?" she smiled. "This is just what I needed. You can't imagine!"

We may feel that we are putting on a good front that fools people into thinking we have it all together; but more often than not, our too-hectic schedules and our frazzled demeanors give us away. People usually notice when our lives aren't running as smoothly as they could.

I have found that, when a person goes through The Grid, the results can speak volumes into their souls and minds. Summing up their day to day life—on paper—helps them begin to see who and what receives their best. It helps them look forward to putting together a plan to make their visions a reality.

After Carrie acknowledged where her time went, she needed to address some personal issues that she didn't even realize she had. Some of her personal needs and responsibilities were being inadvertently ignored, and I completely understood the tendency. During that crazy time of my life when I worked so hard with the students, I came to a point where I realized I was not taking care of me. A walk through the Personal Investment Sectors helped me face the music playing in my life. They reminded me that I have a body to care for, family members to love, and friends to enjoy. Bills needed to get paid and my home needed management. I have passions and talents that need to be encouraged and brought to life, and I have a soul in need of nourishment, too.

When the Personal Life Sectors exercise was placed before Carrie and she circled those areas receiving her attention, she also automatically noticed those that were not. I didn't have to say a word. The list before her did most of the talking.

TAKING INVENTORY

Each of our lives is unbalanced in its own way. You may struggle with watching too much television, while someone else may wrestle with too frantic a social life. I know I need to be exercising regularly, but I find myself spending that time online or chatting on the phone with friends. In any case, the point of the Life Sectors exercise is not to focus us on what we're doing wrong but to show us where we can improve.

Consider Carrie's situation. My friend realized she'd neglected herself in many areas. Five particularly caused concern: Friends, Health/Body, Hobbies, Career, and Dreams. In hopes of helping Carrie get back on track, we took a closer look at each "neglected" zone and set some goals for how she could realistically improve in it.

> Don't worry about what's wrong. Focus on what you can improve.

Friends

A single gal's circle of friends, many times, becomes a type of fill-in family. If you've ever seen episodes of the sit-coms *Friends* or *Seinfeld*, you have witnessed that concept in action. Single gals, however, can become so busy with need-tos and have-tos that we don't even realize when we are slowly shutting out the people we need most. We may not realize when we are not nurturing friendships with other like-minded girls. Schedules, jobs, and responsibilities must not take the place of friends. As poet John Donne wisely wrote, "No man is an island." I'd like to add that no woman is an island either. We girls can't cut ourselves off from companionship.

Carrie was down to almost zero interactions with friends. I challenged her to target just one person that week. Someone who was her age, whom she could plan to meet for coffee. If that was not doable, she could just call that girlfriend and talk. At the very least, they needed to make a phone date. Every girl needs to stay connected.

> Carrie's Goal: Reconnect with someone my own age this week that I enjoy spending time with. Schedule time to chat or get together. Make it happen.

Health/Body

We hear a lot these days about the importance of exercise and nutrition, but these topics are way more than a passing fad. Taking care of our physical health makes us feel better, gives us more energy, and protects us against illness. Similarly, the way we take care of our appearance—think grooming, not plastic surgery—contributes to the way we feel about ourselves overall.

Carrie had let a lot of things go, and one of them was her hair. She has this incredible long, thick mane of hair. It touches the back of her thighs. That hair requires upkeep and maintenance but going to the salon was no longer on her radar.

> Carrie's Health/Body Goal: Schedule a haircut. Get it on my calendar, and take it from there.

Hobbies

Hobbies are important. They help us to de-stress and give us something to look forward to at the close of a long day. Some see hobbies as a form of therapy, and I tend to agree.

Carrie loved to bake. But she had not been able to of late for obvious reasons. A special birthday was coming up that week, and she talked about how she was planning to make her friend dinner and then bake this person's favorite dessert.

> Carrie's Hobbies Goal: Don't worry about making them dinner. Bring home McDonald's, if I have to, but make

that favorite family recipe! Dig it out tonight, and lay it on the counter.

Career

Many of us do what we do for a living, but, deep down, desire a different career. A New York Times best-selling author originally had a typical day job that required an eighty-minute commute to and from work. This job was simply his paycheck. His heart and passion were in writing. So while working away to pay the bills during the day, he used his travel time by train and time during his off hours to work on his dream job. After publishing a little book titled, *The Shack*, his dream came true.

Some of us work toward that dream job in *our* off hours; but for Carrie, there weren't any off hours to devote to that purpose. She simply thought her future dreams and goals would all fall into place as life went on and if she kept working hard. I assured her that would not be the case.

"You have to make life happen or life happens to you." I reminded. She knew it was true. We talked through the desires of her heart and began to discuss what decisions she could make in that direction. One thought, one decision at a time. By achieving this, we would at least get her headed down a path *she* was choosing to walk, rather than one she was being forced to take.

Carrie's Career Goal: Find one person in the field of personal training who I will call and schedule a meeting with this month.

Dreams

We all have dreams—things deep down inside that we want to accomplish in our lives. Our dreams may include a trip to Antarctica, the next great best-selling novel that we have in our heads and would love to pen, running the Boston marathon, or shopping for that new wardrobe to celebrate a drop in four dress sizes.

Carrie knew what she wanted, and she was very driven. She had a lot of dreams and quite a few goals. What surprised me was how she somehow felt they would all magically fall into place "somewhere down the road." She believed that, as long as she kept forging ahead, everything would work out in time. Once we spelled out her dreams on paper, however, she realized that she needed to choose one goal and focus on it for the present. That led her to begin to consider a strategic plan that would head her in that direction.

> *Carrie's Dreams Goal: Write down one dream this week, and figure out what immediate steps I can take to help it become a reality.*

A year after our discussion, Carrie and I discovered that she had created an entirely new life. She landed a full-time, paying situation in a plush side of town near her home. And, she was proud to announce, it was her dream job. She had located a new church, was spending time with friends, and looked about five years younger to boot. Carrie felt like a whole new girl.

Take another look at the Personal Investment Sectors on page 137. In the following section, I've included basic ideas on how to bring each sector back into balance. Think about those areas where you tend to neglect yourself, and then start putting one of these goals into practice.

Remember, small steps can lead to a big payoff.

Career Goal:	Research your field of interest. Find out what you need to do, or who you need to contact, to help you reach your dream job.
Charities/ Outreach Goal:	Help out at the local Rescue Mission or donate to Goodwill. Begin gathering information and items this week!
Dreams Goal:	Contact someone who can help you price out your dream.
Family Goal:	Check travel rates and begin to track specials that will allow you more time with loved ones.
Finances Goal:	Make a savings plan and set aside ten dollars this week to kick off the fund.
Friends Goal:	Call a friend to sync your calendars and make plans to go to dinner together.
Health/Body Goal:	Want to lose five pounds by Christmas? Go to that Zumba class tomorrow night!

Hobbies Goal: Work on your hobby of choice tonight instead of watching television.

Home Life Goal: Make a weekly chores chart. Dust on Monday. Laundry on Tuesday …

Job/Paycheck Goal: Attend a networking meeting or volunteer for a project that can get you on your manager's radar.

Self Improvement/ Education Goal: Call the local community college for class prices. Figure out how to work it into your schedule.

Social Life Goal: Get yourself out there. Call a friend and ask her to join you for a night of dancing.

Spiritual Enrichment Goal: Ask a friend or colleague to visit a new worship center with you this weekend.

Chix Chat:

1. What Personal Life Sector gets the most of your attention?
2. Which sector would you like to give more of your time, energy, or resources?
3. Consider the sector you most neglect. Who do you know who manages that sector well in her own life? Ask her to meet with you. Have her share tips or suggestions on how she makes that sector work for her.
4. If you could only change one thing about the way you focus your energy, what would it be?
5. Name one area of your life that you don't give the proper attention it needs. What can you do to change?

Chapter 16

Going for the Gold

"Many people die with their music still in them. Too often it is because they are always getting ready to live. ... Before they know it ... time runs out."
— Oliver Wendell Holmes

EVER noticed that days can seem interminable, but years seem to fly past? I also find it fascinating how a day filled with fun ends so much more quickly than another day at the office. Most of us live by the clock, always wishing for more hours to do such and such and less to do this or that. But each of us must realize that, while the number of minutes in a day is static, our approach to them should be fluid.

Within each day are a zillion things that demand our attention and many things that need it. Each of us wants to make the most out of our days, but how do we go about it?

You owe it to yourself to get a clear assessment of where you are in your life: what are you doing, and where are you going? As we've learned, not having a clear direction in your approach to life usually leads to the town of Lost. Not having a good handle on how to get the most mileage out of your day leads to the city of Burnout.

In the last chapter, I mentioned my friend Carrie, whose schedule and routine had gotten so jam-packed with extra work and commuting that she'd forgotten about the importance of remembering to dream. When I sat down with Jenny—always the practical no frills girl—I expected to hear that her life was busy, but well-ordered. I expected she had a firm handle on the direction her life was headed. And sure enough, a walk through The Grid and The Weekly

Assessment revealed that she lived by a plan. But once she filled out Monday's schedule, she just copied that into all the other days and sighed.

Her schedule consisted of work, housework, and cooking. She made trips to the gym and the grocery store, but that was about it. Time spent with friends was apparently so miniscule it didn't merit mention.

"Well, Jenny," I said, surprised that she didn't seem to think her routine odd, "have you ever considered changing up your week a bit? Maybe, let some of the cleaning go?"

"I already do," she responded quickly, "I watch TV. Every night."

TIME BUSTERS AND ENERGY WASTERS

How many times have you heard people claim that they just get more done when they're really busy? Often after such a declaration, I roll my eyes and think, *Here we go again.* I am always amazed when people are shocked to find that, the more they have to do, the more they get done. People don't seem to realize that the reason behind this ability is simply focus.

I remember a college roommate who apologetically informed me of her daily rituals and routines. I was impressed, but she was a bit embarrassed by her schedule. Kelly always looked great, got a lot done, and even managed a great social life; so I never understood the problem. But now, I realize that, in keeping to such a rigid way of doing things, Kelly was sometimes unable to enjoy the opportunities and new adventures which life brings. When people are too rigid and unwilling to break their routines, they can miss out.

On the flipside, those who plant themselves in front of the television set might miss out on some great things life has to offer as well. Sometimes, I sit down to catch a few minutes of a show and am shocked two hours later to realize it's time to head to bed. Each time this happens, the dishes are still in the sink, the vacuuming didn't happen, and that bill never got paid. I sacrifice a clean home and peace of mind for too much television.

A few years back, I made a deal with myself. If I watch television, I have to be doing something. Especially during any and every commercial. Exercise, clean, organize. Doesn't matter. If I sit down with that remote, I make sure I have a project that I can engage in as well.

More than television threatens my productivity. The phone is a huge killer of time. A simple call can easily turn into an hour if I'm not careful. Time just gets away from me. Many times, when I take a call, I either ask the caller if I can put them on speaker, or I just wear a headset. That way, I can sweep, pick up, and fold while I'm chatting. I don't want to miss what the caller is saying, but I know that I need to get stuff done.

Surprisingly, I've also discovered that commutes don't have to be time drains. While it's a little tough to multi-task when I'm driving—and of course I should stay focused on the road—plane and train rides are among my favorite opportunities for getting my reading, writing, and research done. A favorite job I once held had me calling on accounts in New York and in D.C. The Amtrak ride between the two cities was the best office time I ever had. I would sit down with my laptop in my departing station and before, I knew it, we were pulling in at my destination. Hours seemed like minutes, and the work I got accomplished was always monumental. Nothing like getting work done while on the go.

WEEKLY ASSESSMENT

In the last chapter, I shared examples from my friend's Personal Life Sectors Assessment. Now it's your turn! This exercise is purposed to help girls understand where they actually invest time each week. "Why bother with this kind of brain work?" you ask. Because you, my dear, are worth it. The Grid shows you who and what receives your time, your energy, and your resources: it highlights where those precious resources are really going. The Personal Life Sectors Assessment shows which areas of your personal life are neglected or need some extra attention. The Weekly Assessment tool gives you a glimpse into the glitches in your personal calendar and your social life—or lack thereof.

Across a sheet of paper, horizontally list the seven days of the week. Under each heading, list things that routinely occupy your time each day. I find it helpful to break my day into time blocks: early a.m., morning, early afternoon, afternoon, early evening, evening, and late night.

I'VE INCLUDED AN EXAMPLE FROM MY WEEK:

Saturday
Early a.m.: Up and at em.
Morning: Write new blog. Update Twitter. Do a bit of cleaning.
Early Afternoon: Off to exercise class.
Afternoon: Back at house. Work on bills and budget. Catch up on reading.
Early Evening: Work on latest paperwork.
Early Evening: Call my mom. Walk the dog.
Evening: Get ready and head out to time with a friend.
Late Evening: Catch up on e-mails and check online sites one last time.

MAKING THE MOST OUT OF EACH DAY

Congratulations! You should now hold an unbiased, honest look at what the logistics of your week really look like. Now, to get the most out of this little exercise, consider adjustments you might need to make.

Look for the non-negotiables in your routine. Where are opportunities for flexibility? Where or what could you feasibly streamline? Are you going out of your way today for something you actually could do on a different day? If given permission to change only one thing about any given day, what would it be? Who would you need to talk to, or what would you need to have happen in order to make that adjustment? What parts of your day would be negatively affected if you made that change? What parts of your day would be affected positively? And most importantly: Will this particular item really matter five years from now?

Once you honestly answer those questions for each day of your week, you will know what you need to do. You will know if you're on the right track or if you need to flip the switches. This type of self analysis puts you back at the controls—right where you belong.

DON'T PUT IT OFF

Every girl has days when she comes home and wants nothing more than to burrow in the covers and forget the last eighteen hours. But if you routinely end your days feeling crummy, there's a reason. Take out a pad of paper, go make a cup of coffee or that special tea you've been saving, sit down, and take out your Grid. Then locate your Personal Investment Sectors sheet and your Weekly Assessment. Go over them one at a time. Tweak them as needed. It won't take long before you see exactly what bothers you the most or what just isn't working in your life. When we're down or feeling blue, we need to get up and keep moving forward.

We get where we want to go by taking baby steps in the direction we need to head. Remember, no one is going to get you and me to our goals. The people in our lives are working on their goals, their lives, and their families. You and I can, and must, invest in our own.

While writing this book, I had to make some tough decisions. Time that I would have liked to spend with family and friends was put on hold. Certain financial opportunities were bypassed. But I had a goal. My lower left quadrant had hold of me like a dog with a bone and wouldn't let go. In order to complete my goal, I had to focus and commit.

> *When you're down or feeling blue, get up, and keep moving forward!*

If I can do it, you can, too. Whatever you want to achieve in life, Girlfriend, I hope you'll go for the gold!

Chix Chat:

1. What day of the week is your busiest? Your most flexible? Your favorite?
2. What one thing particularly stood out to you about your week?
3. What is your least favorite day of the week? Why? How could you practically improve the day?
4. What things would you like to change about your week?

Part 5

Living Large

CHAPTER 17

Golden Girls

"Time and Tide wait for no man, but time always stands still for a woman of thirty."
—Robert Frost

EXERCISES in time management and personal evaluation go a long way in helping my friends and me navigate the swirly waters of singleness. I must admit, though, that big sources of encouragement continue to be historical, as well as, modern-day personalities, and even a few of those TV types, who swam these shark-infested waters before me, both surviving and thriving in the single seas!

You may recall the hit television show from the 1980s, *The Golden Girls*. The sitcom featured four, older single gals who shared their golden years together. These women, with differing personalities (and the ability to drive each other crazy), found that their friendships trumped any problems they faced. Their loyalty to one another kept viewers rooted to their story each week. The show revealed what women, sans men, could do when they join forces and stand together.

Characters like Blanche, Dorothy, Sophia, and Rose became a new set of role models for those of us not sharing a household with a spouse. They reminded us that we do not only survive, but that we can triumph and overcome. When we met these women, we found them coming into their own after the men in their lives departed. The running theme behind the show was that single women are never really alone when they surround themselves with like-minded girls. And, too, that, together, single gals can form family units of their own.

STAR-STUDDED SINGLES

You and I are part of a growing family of girls who are learning to handle our current lives without men. Other well-known women, past and present, have gone on to reach for their gold without a man by their sides. Vision, passion, and drive called many a golden girl to keep moving in the direction of her goals until she either attained them or died trying.

Queen Elizabeth I never married, and she became the most famous and beloved monarch of England. Though the British Parliament begged her to find a husband, Elizabeth reportedly remained a virgin until her death. Her last courtship ended when she was forty-eight years old. The lucky man? François, Duke of Anjou, who was twenty-two years her junior! Though she helped to establish the English Protestant church, she is most remembered for defeating the invincible Spanish Armada. Good Queen "Bess" not only survived, but thrived, in a male dominated society.

> Single girls often form family units of their own.

Joan of Arc was another fascinating single gal. Joan commanded the French Army during a time when a woman was viewed merely as the bearer of children. Joan, however, didn't even like to wear women's clothing and was a warrior at heart. She led the French to several important victories in the Hundred Years' War, but was so controversial that they burned her alive on the stake at the age of nineteen! She was later canonized and made a saint.

Particularly intriguing to me are the single women of history who've made great strides in building the social and spiritual welfare of those in their circles of influence. Missionary **Amy Carmichael** never married, but she went to India with a heart for children and saved uncountable lives through her service. Few know **Henrietta Mears**. A Bible educator and founder of a publishing company, she influenced many people—the most famous among them Billy Graham—through her teaching and testimony. Largely because of Mears's involvement in his life, Graham went on to counsel not only Presidents, but world leaders, and ministered to countless millions. **Mother Teresa** too had a commitment to and affect upon people that was staggering. These girls were world changers.

Of course, many contemporary women are a credit to single girls everywhere, too. **Condoleezza Rice** was the first American black female to become Secretary of State under President George W. Bush. She has not yet married and, at the age of fifty-four, has no children. She speaks fluent Russian, is a concert pianist—even performing for the current Queen of England—and is an accomplished ice skater. Condi traveled the world, speaking to foreign leaders and serving as an ambassador for our country. This woman has created a beautiful, exciting life for herself.

Oprah—that famous woman who needs little introduction—is a media mogul and international celebrity. Born into poverty and raised by a single mother, Oprah became a millionaire by the age of thirty-two. She rose through the ranks of radio and television to become a mega-successful talk-show host and conquered the publishing and film worlds along the way. At one point, she owned homes and estates in eight locations around the world, but her philanthropic gestures are what she will be remembered for most. Oprah's Angel Network has raised millions for the underprivileged and has built hundreds of homes for victims of Hurricane Katrina. She also established the Oprah Winfrey Leadership Academy for Girls near Johannesburg, South Africa. She too has never married and has no surviving children.

Sarah Duchess of York, radio host Laura Ingraham, author Anne Coulter, and publisher Arriana Huffington are other unmarried ladies in the spotlight. Actresses Cameron Diaz, Drew Barrymore, Teri Hatcher, Penelope Cruz, Kirstie Allie, Jennifer Aniston, Keira Knightley, Doris Day, Elizabeth Taylor, and Anne Hathoway are also single as of this writing. Musicians Madonna, Britney Spears, Whitney Houston, Tina Turner, and both Naomi and Wynonna Judd are single. Socialite Paris Hilton is still sans spouse as well. The list goes on.

A MAN DOESN'T EQUAL HAPPILY EVER AFTER

Acknowledging famous single ladies does more than remind us that we are not alone. Their stories are touching examples of the fact that while beautiful women may long for a man to call their own, the hands of fate do not always play in our favor.

I'm reminded of Katherine Hepburn's story. The beautiful 1940s actress never married her beloved fellow screen star, Spencer Tracy, who was married to another woman during their entire affair. In fact, the day came when Hepburn found herself sitting outside in her car down the street from his funeral.[1] While the star surely grieved her circumstances over the course of her life, she was willing to love and commit to a man whose wife never granted a divorce. But she certainly didn't allow her personal life to affect her success.

Hepburn managed four Oscars for Best Actress, with twelve additional nominations. In addition, she won an Emmy Award (plus four other nominations), two Tony Awards, and eight Golden Globes. In 1999, the American Film Institute ranked Hepburn as the greatest female star in the history of American cinema. Not bad for a single gal.

Jacqueline Kennedy Onassis was single longer than she was married. Her marriage to Jack Kennedy was only ten years long, and her marriage to Onassis lasted but seven years. Of her sixty-five years of life, Jackie was only married for seventeen. A widow for the second time by age forty-six, Jackie accepted a position as an editor and entered the literary and publishing world. She also had a passion for the preservation and protection of America's cultural heritage. Aside from her famous renovation of the White House while First Lady, she was part of a campaign to save and renovate Grand Central Terminal. A lesser known fact is that she is also credited with the saving of several temples and objects of Egyptian antiquity.

Lady Diana is best remembered for her work apart from Prince Charles. Dubbed "The People's Princess," the beloved English Rose was the face of the International Campaign to Ban Landmines. That campaign went on, after her death, to win the Nobel Peace Prize in 1997; many believe it a posthumous tribute to the princess. Though both her relationship with the future king and her own life prematurely perished, Diana is immortalized by her nation and the world.

Each of these amazing gals made an indelible mark on our planet. But not all were blessed with happy hubby endings. Even those women who did walk down the aisle found that their fairy tales did not end as expected. Hollywood and the spotlight provide many examples of how even story book marriages can end badly.

Princess Diana's marriage to Prince Charles provides the best known example of this, but other public figures share similar woes. Marilyn Monroe married three times, but died divorced and alone at the tender age of thirty-six. Lucille Ball remarried after life with Desi Arnaz, but her divorce from her Latin lover indirectly found its way into her later television series, where she was always cast as a single woman.

A ring on the finger does not come complete with an insurance policy guaranteeing a traditional happily ever after. I am a fan of marriage, but I do realize it is a union of two fallible people who have to commit to make it work. Marriage can and should be a wonderful thing. But so can being single. Single isn't so unusual, and I hope you've come to see. It simply happens to the best of us.

Understanding that singleness can and does happen, don't be surprised if thirty years from now Kathy Griffin, Jennifer Aniston, Kate Winslet, and Pink are found sharing a walk up in Manhattan. Who knows. They might just talk themselves into making a hilarious *Golden Girls* remake. If they do, I'm betting we'll all tune in to watch.

Chix Chat:

1. Name one single female who you feel is a good role model. What do you admire about her?
2. What single female character do you enjoy watching on television? Why?
3. Name one famous single you consider successful. What has earned her that place in your mind?
4. If you could be remembered for one particular success, what would it be? Why?

CHAPTER 18

Single Is a Subculture

"Both of you are birds of self-same feather."
—*William Shakespeare*

WHEN I started plotting the outline of this book, I quickly recognized that the term *single* can mean oh-so-much! As you saw in the previous list of well-known women and in my family tree, those who are divorced, widowed, and not-yet-married all use this designation. In my grandmother's day, a divorced-woman was never referred to as single again, but times have changed. Nowadays, "single" comes in various shapes and sizes and from a variety of backgrounds. And the truth, I think, is that our subculture has grown so complicated that certain sectors of society don't quite know what to do with us.

Church groups, synagogues, and even certain community programs struggle with this ever-growing people group. When they invite single girls into a room, they often encounter several—if not all—of the following subgroups:

- Those who've never married
- The formerly married (divorced)
- Those who are widowed
- Single parents
- Those who are separated (legally married but living a single lifestyle)
- Homosexuals

Recently, a group of girls and I sat around a table with two sponsors who were pleased with their new venture of starting up a singles department at my church.

"Let's meet on Sunday night," suggested a professional gal who sat across the table from me.

"No way," the woman to my left quickly retorted, "If we meet on Sunday evenings, there will be no child care! Sunday mornings is the best option!"

I, a mere dog owner, sat in silence. I didn't live in her world, and I didn't think about childcare before I went out. But suddenly, it seemed that most everyone in the room had a very strong opinion on when we should meet; and few coincided.

The sponsors, who sincerely thought they were creating a new single's community to reach *every* single, found themselves facing more dilemmas than had crossed their minds.

"Hey, I get it," one of the sponsors finally said—likely desperate to relate and solve the mess—"I was single. I didn't marry until I was—twenty-five!"

Every never-been-married forty-something in the room froze. We didn't know whether to laugh out loud or stone him for his ignorance; but, I am pleased to report, he survived

Well meaning men and women across the country, if not the world, are truly trying to reach out to the single domain; but they often see singleness as a mess we got ourselves into and a problem they must help us fix. And fast. A few hope we will come to accept the supposed gift of singleness and embrace it with grace. But they can't know how most of us feel about that "single as a gift" concept. "Does this gift come with a return policy?" I always want to ask, "Because, if it does, I'd sure like to send it back!"

Anyone interested in creating a singles group, club, or community of sorts is in for a lot more than they initially bargained for or planned. Well-intended organizations think they know how to help, but the entire spouseless scenario comes with twists and stories they seldom grasp. While hosting a singles group used to be based around a simple idea of introducing folks to others in the market for a spouse, the new dynamics and requirements are enough to make any organizer's or ministry leader's head spin.

The old method of putting singles in a room and hoping they'll hurry up and marry each other has passed. But since many organizations continue to mold their programs around this model, more and more people who find themselves suddenly and dramatically single don't know where to turn. The number of single girls looking for safe, positive, and enjoyable places to meet potential mates encounter an ever-increasing challenge. Many just no longer care for or want any part of the bar scene.

We don't need yet another religious or community sponsored dating service. Single girls just want a place to belong and call our own. A place where the people in the room speak our language and understand our unique subculture. My friend Sandy put it this way, "Places of worship [especially] are family oriented, which is right and proper, but they don't know what to do with us singles. When others introduce themselves and talk about what they do and how long they've been married, I say that I've been single fifty years and worked overseas. Then they don't pity me; instead, they're interested in me."

Sandy both sums up the problem and offers the solution: Places of worship, clubs, and organizations know what to do with the couples and the children in their midst. They know how to reach out to them and speak their language. They want to meet their needs. And they are committed to creating programs for them. Odd, however, that the ever growing single population rarely even finds its own line item placed in the budgets of these well meaning institutions.

GOOD TO KNOW ...

I've done a lot of thinking on this topic, and I've come to believe that the main challenge worship centers and organizations face in reaching singles is that their ministry to us is often run by married people.

The women's ministry leader at my church is married but is genuinely concerned about creating a community at our church for singles. During a recent discussion, she commented to me that she feels amazed by the beautiful, talented, and spiritually devoted single women she knows.

Hoping to help her better understand our demographic, I asked, "Do you feel that way about the single men you know? Are you surrounded by handsome, talented, well-traveled, professional men who are well versed in the Scriptures and are committed to serving Christ?"

She looked blank for a moment before admitting, "You know, Stephanie, I can't think of any."

As I watched, she continued to struggle to come up with at least one name. But she couldn't. I felt I had helped her make an important connection. The first thing those who effectively want to reach out to singles must know is this: the nice, educated, and attractive women who join clubs and groups and then work to become a part of them are not oddities and they've done nothing wrong.

These days, I wish I could give every well-meaning spiritual advisor, civic leader or institution the following pointers on reaching out to our very unique and savvy demographic:

1. More single women than men will participate in group or club activities. Plan accordingly.
2. The worship service can be the loneliest time of the week. Consider creating an optional seating area for the single crowd. Be sure that they are made aware of it.
3. Many women these days are well educated, cultured, and have traveled the nation, if not the globe. Don't make any assumptions about a woman just because she's unmarried.
4. Many single women are continually made to feel inferior or "marked" if they have not successfully landed a man by a certain age. Be sensitive to this fact.
5. Single girls don't want to be judged or condemned for being strong. Take care not to penalize or punish them for taking on life's challenges and surviving them without the help of spouses. Encourage them to use their wealth of knowledge, personal drives, and their passionate pursuit of things important to them.
6. The notion that single women are too picky is just not valid. Avoid using any reference to it.
7. Avoid saying to girls, "Let Jesus be your husband." People never say to single men, "Let Jesus be your wife."
8. Many women raised in families of faith were told, "If you are a good girl, and love God, He will bring you a wonderful man." When that doesn't happen, they feel very confused, frustrated, and let down.
9. Few singles need to hear people quote scriptures about the perks of singleness. They simply need hugs.
10. Single women need someone to call when the plumbing leaks or the car breaks down. Try to create a support group to meet such needs.
11. Single girls need people to ask how they are doing. While they may not answer honestly for fear that they will be seen as a whiny inconvenience, they'll be grateful for the interest.

12. Many single women have an incredible passion for life. They want to live life and live it large. They just need some encouragement and support.

The best way a singles' organizer or club leader can earn a single gal's respect is to get to know, not just our demographic and its complexities, but us personally and to understand our current lifestyle.

For instance: most of us are grateful for the life we lead. While we'd like to marry, we just need encouragement during this season of our lives. Further, we don't want to be punished for being strong and doing the best with our lives that we could. In no way do we wish to be remembered as bitter women who did not get the house with the picket fence, the two-car garage, and the 1.5 kids playing in the yard with a family dog. Instead, we want to be known as the girls who made the best of the hand they were dealt as they looked for ways to create successful and happy lives.

I want to be known as someone who did my part in my corner of the world. I want to be known as the woman who truly aimed to be a good woman. A responsible citizen. A loyal family member. A hard-worker. And an educated individual. Most importantly, I want to be a worthy role model to those lovely young ladies who will come after me.

The girls in my circle would likely adopt that last paragraph as their own. It reflects who we are. It explains what we have to offer. And it says what we would like to share with every community organizer, to each concerned organization, and to the world.

Chix Chat:

1. Describe a singles group or organization you recently attended. What did you like about it? How could it have been better?
2. If you belong to a singles group or organization, explain your involvement.
3. Why are you or are you not involved in a group geared toward singles?
4. If you could organize your own singles club, what would it look like? Who would you involve? What activities would you plan?

CHAPTER 19

The No Sex in the City Club

"What is conservatism? Is it not adherence to the old and tried, against the new and untried?"
—Abraham Lincoln

MY friend Jeri refers to the subject of this chapter as "the elephant in the room" and insisted that I get it out there. And so, after a very long evening pouring over my notes and trying to avoid writing about this topic all together, here I go. This is my sex chapter or—perhaps more appropriately—my accepted lack thereof.

A while back, a friend sent me an e-mail with the subject heading, "Strange Request." As I opened it, I realized that she was really asking me for a favor. She hoped I'd be willing to embark on an "opportunity" of sorts. A well-known media outlet was looking to interview older singles who did not participate in sex outside of marriage. By choice.

My friend who received the initial e-mail is much like me: single, not-yet married, and approximately of the same age range. A more important similarity in this instance is that we both hold a belief that sex was designed by God specifically for marriage. (Yes, you heard me right.) Believe it or not, we as modern, educated, professional women are committed to "waiting."

Knowing that the "holding out" topic isn't popular these days, I wondered if I was really up for the task. My grandmother always asked me, "Why should a man buy the cow if the milk's free?" And I believed in the soundness of her logic. But did the New York media set really want to hear quaint advice from little ole me? I wasn't so sure.

I noted that the original e-mail came from a freelance writer for a well-known publication. She was on the hunt for talkative singles and was doing research to prove an unpopular point; but how does an interviewer go about asking folks nationwide to admit they intentionally don't have sex? I was fully aware that the powers that be in the metropolitan base could not fathom the idea that the abstinent species even exist in this twenty-first century environment. I knew in my heart, however, that many women out there hold the same views I share with my friends. I couldn't pass up my chance to say to them, "You, my dear, are not alone. And there are more of us out there than you ever imagined!"

DEAR WORLD: I RESERVE THE RIGHT TO ABSTAIN

If I had to rate my interview experience, I'd give it a five out of ten. The girl asking the questions wasn't too thrilled with her assignment, and she definitely was not chomping at the bit to hear my ridiculous reasons for imposed intimate inactivity. I got through it and assumed that would be the end of it.

But no sooner had our chat begun to fade from my memory than the phone rang. A radio station's producer wanted to know if I'd be willing to talk about my lifestyle choice on the air. I have to admit; I had a moment of panic over the thought, but I agreed to do it all the same.

I immediately called my friend who had gotten me into the mess in the first place by sending me the "Strange Request" e-mail. I told her, "You're meeting me for coffee, now. This public relations stuff is your world, not mine. You have to coach me on how to do this interview."

A couple of hours over coffee and some great notes later, I prepared to take the national plunge.

A LIFESTYLE OF CHOICE

Soon I announced to the world that I am a woman who has chosen a lifestyle of waiting. While I certainly don't pass judgment on those who don't share my views, I do hope to affirm those who do. Sitting in my home office gripping the phone with both hands, I let the world in on a few interesting facts:

1. **We "abstainers" are not an extinct species.**
   Though our culture and the media no longer hold to the values that once drove the nation, some of us are "non-conformists" or modern day rebels. We don't live according to peer pressure, and we don't give

away our assets; instead, we intentionally withhold them for the man willing to commit to us for life.

True, our species is endangered. But not only are we very much alive, we are living well.

2. **Abstinence is nothing to feel embarrassed over.**

    Many women make the choice to wait. Some hope to wait for true love and the implied security of a wedding band. Some fear pregnancy or STDs. Some even make the decision to abstain for religious reasons. But the vast majority of us would check several of the above and say that we're also glad to go against the popular tide that says everybody oughta be doing it.

    Though it's not in vogue and the media would die if they discovered the truth, our commitment of choice shouldn't be that much of a shock. Withholding used to be the norm.

3. **We modern day "waiters" didn't invent abstinence.**

    For centuries abstinence was not only *ex*pected, it was actually *re*spected. The Sexual Revolution didn't really surface until about fifty years ago. Before that, abstaining was the preferred choice of most. Furthermore, for hundreds of years nuns and many priests have chosen to abstain from sex throughout their entire lives. While we've all heard stories about the secret passageways and underground tunnels connecting nunneries and monasteries, not all members of the celibate communities are sexually active in secret. You may not hear about these holy people and their decent lifestyles in History 101 or see them headlining in any movies or documentaries, but they have existed and still do!

OUT OF THE MOUTHS OF—MEN?

Not long ago most girls could look to their wedding nights with a little old-fashioned excitement, naiveté, and nervousness. Nowadays, girls have magazines, websites, books, and blogs that show them how to not only attract but please their man of the hour.

Whatever your story or experience, understand that some attractive, intelligent, and completely sane women out there are holding firm and holding out; and there's nothing wrong with them for doing so. If you have chosen or wish to choose a path of waiting, know that you are not alone. You are not a freak of nature. You were designed to be cherished and protected.

What I hadn't expected or anticipated in agreeing to share my story was the incredible grace and respect I received from the producer and from both of the radio hosts. Not only did they support my decision, they applauded it. The unmarried producer even commented on air—in a very respectful tone—that he hoped he lived up to my expectations. It was as if the crew was somehow refreshed to know that a few ladies out there are still willing to wait.

A few days later, I answered the phone only to find that I was, yet again, live and on-the-air. My friend's hunch that I would be "sabotaged live" during this revealing process came to fruition. The hard-rock station's rough, mostly male audience had callers waiting in line, on-hold, ready and willing to graphically tell me how they could help me solve my waiting "problem."

I was pleasantly surprised, however, to find the hosts slowly moving from feeding me to the wolves to hanging up on lewd callers and defending me! It was surreal.

As soon as we ended the call, I contacted my webmaster to warn him that we might get hit hard with ugly comments regarding my latest on-air time. I'd done my best to field the comments wisely, but I was aware of the reality that I might be harassed over my decision to speak out against the norm.

Thankfully, the mean and nasty e-mails never came. I was shocked to realize when it was all said and done that I had not received one negative response to my stance. Not one! Instead, men e-mailed me in support, pouring out their hearts and encouraging me to stay strong and hold out. While I had a few invitations for dates in the midst of the feedback, most of the comments came from men wishing that they too could adopt or return to an abstinence mentality and lifestlye:

> *Stephanie, morning. Just wanted to say that I enjoyed listening to you yesterday morning. You have a marvelous speaking voice and an interesting message. Your attitude is refreshing. — Keep smiling, M.*

> *I have had the same girlfriend for the last 6 years and hopefully next year I'll get up the courage to ask her to marry me. My only regret has*

> been that, had I known I was going to meet her, I would have waited to have sex. I just wanted to say that I am happy for you to be able to be so strong. It must be hard in this world of sex-saturated media and music. Congratulations on staying strong and focused on your goal.—*Truly,* D.

> I am divorced with 4 grown children ... In some ways, [waiting] makes me feel as if I am an outcast. How will women look at my commitment of celibacy? —D.

> [Many] cannot comprehend your "choice" for abstinence ... in today's world. I commend you for so bravely sharing your testimony of purity ... especially under their negative and rude perspectives! You were so awesome! Even your silence on their one remark was magnificent ... [it steered] the conversation back into their respect of you. —R.

I was very touched and appreciated the kind remarks, but I found myself thinking that these men who apparently wanted better for themselves were listening to what was typically a foul radio show. A show that presented women as little more than disposable sex toys. Items of mere pleasure. It made me wonder if maybe some of the same pressure the entertainment industry places on girls to give it up might also be somewhat responsible for encouraging men—even some of the best ones—to claim a woman's body as a prize deserved. One man in the media world confessed to me privately, "[Having sex] was the monkey on my back. One New Year's Eve I said to myself, 'the first girl I meet that is willing, I'm doing it. I'm going to get this over with.'"

BRAGGING RIGHTS, OR MAYBE NOT

Shortly after my interviews, I met Rezando. Rezie, as he is known to his friends, owns a limousine service in the outskirts of a famous metropolitan area. He has never been married, but he does have an eleven-year-old daughter. Rezie prides himself in that, when he was younger, he referred to himself as "the virginizer."

Once during a long drive for which Rezie was my chauffer, I shared my story regarding my lifestyle choice. (Amazing the conversations that come up during a long trip!) When I did, he about drove off the freeway. In the weeks ahead, my new friend—who began calling me just to pick my brain regarding such foreign topics—began sharing with me that he could see that perhaps his past life wasn't all that it was supposedly cracked up to be. Surprisingly, he came to respect my decision; and while he definitely didn't want to match my lifestyle choice, he did decide that maybe it wasn't so "stupid" after all. In fact, it sounded like a perfect idea to present to his daughter as she grew into adulthood.

Though he had lived to conquer young girls, Rezie wanted his girl to remain pure. It was strange to hear him want abstinence for his daughter, while he personally embraced an opposing lifestyle. "The women you sleep with are someone else's daughters too, you know," I once chided. The other end of the phone was eerily silent.

Rezie once suggested early in our talks that my girlfriends and I had made our lifestyle choice due to religion—as if we bear it like a cross or as a requirement—like the vows of chastity one takes to become a monk or nun. I laughed and shared with him that quite a few women in the church today may not openly admit it, but a lot of them don't have any problem with sex outside of marriage. In fact, surveys and statistics prove that relatively few do.

My choice to strive at keeping the act of love making inside marriage is a cognizant, rational decision. It's not merely a spiritual one. It just makes sense to me. The act of sex is not merely physical, but it is deeply emotional, mental, and spiritual. I am not a theologian, and I have no intention of trying to land a television appearance that presents me as an expert on sex. But I have seen more than my share of girls in tears who have given all only to say it wasn't worth it. I have yet to meet a girl that has said, "Stephanie, I am so glad I *didn't* wait. Girls should give it up. And early!"

> *Not merely physical, the act of sex is deeply emotional, mental, and spiritual.*

Waiting can be a good thing. Easy? No. But a better and wiser choice? Definitely, yes.

FOR THOSE WHO HAVE BEEN ABUSED

I want to speak to the precious girls out there who would've loved to have had the opportunity to give themselves to their husbands alone. Sadly, the option is prematurely taken from many. Perhaps you suffered from abuse, and your body was violated. Please hear me. My heart goes out to you, and I would give anything to wipe those horrific memories away and hold your hand.

Please know this. God does not see violation as a lack of purity. I believe sexual purity is something only *you* can give away. If someone took it from you, remember that you never gave it. A person may have taken your body against your will, but you never gave it to them for the purpose of love.

Most of us girls have been going to gynecologists for years. Does that make us loose women? Heavens, no! Were our bodies exposed to male doctors? Yes. Does that mean we are not pure? No. The main difference is that lying naked with a man for the purpose of pleasure and giving yourself to him in the name of love is a very different matter than a physical test or a medical procedure. If you were raped or sexually violated in any way, that was not an act of love-making. That was not love at all.

Jeri, I am sad to say, was violated sexually at an early age. Later in life, after much consternation and experimentation with the world of sex, she realized that, while she couldn't undo what was done to her in her early years, she could've chosen to abstain after the fact. She offers valuable insight on the impact sex has on the dating girl: "Sex offers instant gratification—like a sugar high. It lasts for a moment. Then it's gone. And I still find myself alone."

Television shows, music, movies, and magazines not only educate but tutor our youth and our culture in sexual experiences. Messages from all angles preach the gospel of "Don't deprive yourself of this biological need." All forms of media scream that sex is yours for the taking. An inherent right. Go out there and get it!

But are we truly better off for having so indulged?

OUT OF THE MOUTHS OF BABES

I thought it would be interesting to see what the up and coming generations, who have cut their teeth on a sexually charged society, think about the subject. I pulled out the laptop and began to delve into some current data.

Consider what these young women shared about their decisions to have sex outside of marriage:

I was in love. Yet I felt guilty. —Sandy, 17

I felt cheap [after sex] because I thought about what I did and I realized I wasn't ready for it. —Kara, 16

I felt strange and, in a sense, used. It was like we were both caring for the same person—him. I felt left out of it.—Betsy, 15

I felt angry, I had promised myself I would wait until I was married, but I did it anyway. Now it was too late. I had lost my virginity.—Ande, 15

I knew I had made the biggest mistake of my life. I felt stupid.—Char, 14

I felt as if I had done something wrong. But aside from that, I felt stupid ridiculous. I certainly didn't get any thrill out of it. It was embarrassing to say the least.—Elle, 16 [1]

On the same website young men responded to the following question, "Why do guys often drop a girl soon after having sex with her?" Their answers included the following:

You get bored. It's like a kid with a toy. When he first gets it, he spends all day with it. Then after he breaks it in, it's not fun anymore, so he finds another toy.—Ron, 16

It's just like in the meat market. You just want to go out there and get some fresh meat.—Jack, 19

After I have sex with a girl, I don't care if I see her anymore. —Jorey, 15

After the first time we had sex, we stopped talking. She never called me and I never called her. I thought she was an easy catch because she gave me sex too quickly. —Wade, 15

Sometimes I wish a girl would say no and keep saying no. If we took it slow, we'd probably still be together. —Paul, 17 [2]

YOU'RE A WHAT?!

Though present day culture cannot comprehend it, those of the "waiting kind" persuasion do exist. This was brought to my attention as I was recently introduced to some adorable twenty-somethings in Australia. These healthy, happy lasses proudly proclaimed to me that they have made the choice to wait for marriage. But they didn't stop there. Four of the particular females, living in the land of koalas and kangaroos, confessed to me that they were, indeed, virgins!

Shortly after my time with them, I was lunching with a professional acquaintance in Washington D.C. Oddly enough, our discussion turned to the topic of a book her company was about to release that dealt with sex and our culture. While munching away on our fried catfish and French fries, she posed the question, "Do you really think there *are* any twenty-something virgins out there?" She was dead serious.

Though a professing Roman Catholic herself, she honestly was under the impression that the virgin population on this planet had gone the way of the dinosaur. Taking into account additional private confessions that have come my way, along with my encounter during my hop across the international dateline, I assured her that virgins do in fact exist.

Naturally, I had to wonder what the young people of today had to say about abstinence, let alone virginity. Surprisingly, I found a variety of comments in support of it:

> *It sounds tacky, but I say wait until you're married. Guys have more respect for virgins.* —Sue, 17

> *Wait until you're married. Then when you have sex, it will mean something—that you're in love with your husband and want him to be the first.* —Robin, 17

> *There are a lot of guys who only want one thing, and after that, you're history.* —Cathy, 17

> *Wait until you're married. Most guys out there are users and you'll end up getting hurt, having a bad reputation, and more than likely, in the long run, being alone.* —Lance, 18

If I had it to do over again, I would save my virginity until I was married.
—Vicki, 18 [3]

The world will tell you that sex is fabulous. Proof is everywhere you look. Every person I come in contact with on a daily basis reminds me that two people most likely had a blast during the fateful union that resulted in that new person. Sex is special. It should be. God invented it. And when He creates something, He makes it perfect. Initially. Then we have that amazing knack of messing it up.

I'm concerned that at some point modern society decided that virginity is no longer something to cherish but to get rid of. I wonder: When did we exchange the search for a lifetime of love with that for the search of a moment?

A friend recently shared her hopes for her young daughters: "I want the girls in my family to dream big and beyond their town and their moment. They can have more opportunities if they won't do what their moms did and get pregnant at sixteen."

How right she is! We truly can empower ourselves and improve our futures by saving our bodies from men who are simply looking for a good time and some biological relief.

Our world would be so different were men raised to understand that we have so much more to offer them than just sex. Magazine covers, movies, and more encourage men to think we are but playthings, and sometimes the way we dress only reinforces the notion. Let's be honest: parading around in tiny dresses and bikinis doesn't exactly say, "I can't wait to be the mother of your children."

I CAN'T SAY NO

If you have chosen to give yourself to someone outside of marriage and you're in support of that lifestyle, the above may seem a bit dramatic and over-stated. But here's a little experiment for you. Turn on the television, pick up a magazine, listen to a best-selling CD, or head to the movies. You will get plenty of sex-outside-of-marriage scenarios since few of the couples you'll encounter engaging in a sex act are married, even on screen. Ask yourself, *Are these people truly achieving happiness and finding real fulfillment through their moments of passion? Or are they trading a good thing—like a quick hook up—for a great one—like a lifetime of loving commitment?*

I can't help but thinking of those men who took the time to write to me after that one particular interview. If they found it in themselves to applaud and affirm one girl's choice to abstain, that should be an encouragement to all of us "I don't throw myself out there to just anyone either" ladies.

If you have been strong enough and brave enough to choose a lifestyle of waiting, know that you're not a bizarre oddity. It's my desire to reach out to you and say as much. And who knows, maybe together we can start an underground movement? We shall see. In the meantime, stay strong. Stay true to your heart. Stand firm. And be well.

Chix Chat:

1. What are your thoughts regarding sex outside of marriage?
2. What factors and experiences led you to your current beliefs on the topic?
3. Do you feel relationships that experience sex before marriage are stronger or weaker as a result? Explain.
4. Do you think our current culture is stronger due to the openness regarding the topic of sex? How so?
5. Would your family and friends agree or disagree with your stance regarding sex outside of marriage?
6. If you could share one point on this topic with the world, what would that be? Why?

CHAPTER 20

Starting Your Own Chix Chat Club

"The most exclusive clubs only have a couple members and they're very hard to find."
—Sarah Jessica Parker

THROUGHOUT this book, I've often mentioned my Coffee Klatch of Five—that delightful group of like-minded single gals with whom I share my life and my time. Nothing compares to being with a group of people who accept me for who I am—warts and all. Ah, the joy of simply being allowed to be myself!

In earlier chapters, I suggested you find those like minds and hearts who can help you navigate the single waters of your life. Girls with whom you can best relate, learn from, and even encourage in return. They are out there, and—if you haven't done so already—it's time to find them and start connecting.

Whether you find single friends at work, in your place of worship, or in your social or professional circles, many gals are just waiting for the right group with whom to connect. Quite possibly, your invite will answer someone's prayer.

We girls have lots to say, and we like to say it out loud. Usually, if we can locate a sympathetic, listening ear, we feel much better after a quick vent. Girls need to build a network or community to help one another in practical ways. If, for instance, you have a great handy man, some other single girl probably needs to know about him too. If you recently changed insurance companies and saved money, you might save another single sister hours of research.

CHOOSING CHARTER MEMBERS

Finding like-kinds is the first key to success in starting your own Chix Chat Club. If you are of the not-yet married persuasion, seek out other gals close to your age who share your similar status. If you are divorced, look for women who understand what it's like to deal with that "ex" factor. If single with kids, you will benefit from a group that can discuss the challenges of and exchange ideas for raising children. And too, if you are an executive, you might best benefit from meeting with a group of girls facing similar professional situations. Sure, you can "inter-mix," but there's nothing like sharing your heart with someone who's been in your shoes and "gets it."

Step One: List potential members.

The best way to start the process of club building is to make a list based on your contacts. Start with the names and numbers in your cell or PDA and then go through your e-mail addresses and even your Christmas card and gift lists. Write down the name and contact information of every unattached girl in your circle of influence.

Step Two: Hone your list.

Should you find relatively few savvy single girls within your contacts, don't worry. In fact, my group started with only two and quickly grew. So will yours. Since conversation is the cornerstone of a successful Chix Chat Club, keep the numbers low to ensure each voice is heard. Five is the perfect group size: odd numbers work great in that they avoid too much pairing up and help to break a tie when and if you need to take a vote on deciding where and when to meet next!

Should you need to pare down your initial list, consider these tips. While you want to locate people who will strive together in singleness, the goal of gathering as a group is to help each other towards the state of *thriving*. Sadly, some people just aren't in a position emotionally or mentally to make their own lives better—much less someone else's. No amount of spending time with or listening to such people will change their black hole tendencies. Therefore, it's best not to insist that such people join your group. Remember the "Sappers" from our grid chapters? Those are the ones you probably should avoid.

In addition, you'll want to consider whether each girl on your list would actually *like* to commit to catching up and touching base in this fashion once a month or so. If her schedule gets so crazy, that it will only frustrate everyone; or if she is the kind of person who habitually cancels at the last minute, she will only add stress. Not relieve it.

In general, look for girls who won't dominate all conversation. Seek out people who try to be good listeners. Together, you'll strive to grow and learn and improve. Avoid the sisters who are forever in crises mode or a bit addicted to drama. Remember, the goal of starting a Chix Chat club is to find a group of girls who can, and wish to, help one another thrive. Sounds like a tall order; but believe me, it's doable.

Think chemistry. Decide whether the people on your list share similar education, job, social, or religious beliefs. Remember that if two in a group of three have six figure incomes and the third works a retail register, the women's needs, as well as the conversations they can comfortably share, will differ. Don't invite tension. Instead, put together a list of like minds to help you in your daily life conflicts; who will commit to helping you discover solutions. Plan to learn from and help each other as you go.

While I'm not suggesting that you interview the girls on your lists as if you were looking for a roommate or a business partner, be very picky about who will receive your precious thoughts and feelings down the road. If that girl you're considering is a gossip, she's not likely capable of keeping conversations confidential. If you don't know that she'll have your back, think twice about including her in your new inner circle.

> *Be selective in sharing feelings. Emotions need and deserve a safe place to land.*

In every case, be selective. Your emotions and feelings need and deserve a safe place to land.

Step Three: Know presentation is everything.

When I first started my "club," I could only think of one person who fit my current "like-kinds" wish list. In time, I thought of another three gals who fit the bill. I personally met with or contacted each of them face-to-face. Within a few months, we had set the date to meet together. Not all of the girls knew each other, so it was fun to look forward to introducing them. Going into our first gathering, however, I'd made introductions via e-mail and shared what all we had in common. By the time we joined, they were intrigued and looking forward to meeting other new friends "just like them."

Approaching someone about this type of venture is a bit sensitive, and agreeing to be with a group of other singles for the purpose of encouragement and support is not something to take lightly. Keep in mind as you invite girls to be a part of your club that you want to build a sense of camaraderie with each of them. Be sure that you communicate your wish to keep this new scheme fun. Keep it light. You might not want to present the idea over the phone, via e-mail, text message, or Twitter. Instead, set up a coffee time, lunch, or dinner with each girl—beginning with the person on your list with whom you already feel the best personal connection. This personal approach allows you to relay your message clearly.

As you kick off each of these get-togethers, see how the conversation goes. Talk about how they are handling their current single status, and ask if they've ever considered joining a unique support group for non-married gals. If they seem open to the idea, share about your bright new venture and see if they would like to join. If not, that's okay. We singles aren't looking for more commitments, more meetings, or more pressure. This club needs to be a safe haven and a sanctuary for the weary. Something to look forward to. Something that rejuvenates. No one needs another dent in an already full calendar or another "have-to." The club should invoke smiles, not groans, when mentioned.

Once you find your first member, broach with her the subject of who else might benefit from or fit in your new club. Agree on the next girl who may enjoy being a part, and invite that new person to meet with the two of you to discuss the possibility. (Take care not to pressure the potential person into a commitment. You don't want to feel stuck with her, or each other, until you feel confident that the mix feels right. Check how the chemistry works when the three of you come together.)

If at the end of your first meeting, person number three is a hit, then tell her what you're up to and invite her to join the group. Once your group begins to get together regularly, consider adding other girls by using this approach.

Step Four: Communicate group goals.

Soon after your inaugural Chix Chat gathering, be sure that you've communicated to each person that you're looking to establish a coffee chat environment where like-minded women can come together and talk about surviving and thriving in the midst of singleness. Make sure they know that, while some whining is well and good, you want to encourage one another during your times together. You might even start off your first true Chix Chat by saying, "Hey, there is a good old boys club. What we need is a dynamite single gals club! How can we accomplish that?" Or you can always default to, "Okay, who had the worst day? Winner gets a latte on me!"

When you come together, allow each girl to share what she is going through at work, to talk about the latest project she is working on, or discuss that new situation she is dealing with. Whether family problems or that cute guy down at the gym, allow her to share what's on her heart. Then, ask if she's open to advice on handling that new boss, neighbor, or latest crush. If so, allow each group member a chance to weigh-in.

Remind the girls to focus on encouraging and helping one another. Take care not to pass judgment or discourage; either is rarely helpful. You don't need a women's circle full of weird vibes and competition. Think the Three Musketeers. All for one and one for all.

GUIDELINES ARE GOOD

Once a group begins to officially gather, it doesn't hurt to establish some club guidelines. You can always create your own as you go. The following are a few you might consider trying within your circle:

1. Everyone gets a time to share, whine, cry, or babble.
2. As possible, everyone gets equal chat time.
3. Each girl should help the one most in need at the moment. When it's your turn to respond to a friend's story or struggle, offer some kind of assistance or support. If you can lend some help after you have said your good-nights or good-byes, do so.
4. Make sure the tone does not turn judgmental, and never end your special time together on a negative or sour note. Find a way to leave others encouraged.
5. Designate a point person for your next Chix Chat. (You can rotate.) This volunteer will be the woman who agrees to keep the girls aware of

the calendar, communicate about any scheduling conflicts that might prevent you from meeting, and send out that next reminder, text, or e-mail.
6. Always try to schedule your next time together at the end of your current gathering.
7. Commit to getting together with the group as often as possible—even if you have to conference call or Skype in—do it. Make the club a priority.
8. Network, network, network with each other when you are together and apart.
9. Encourage one another as best as possible. While you can't fix every problem, (and you shouldn't try to do as much) you can be a listening ear and a caring shoulder to lean on—two priceless gifts.
10. Keep it fun. Keep it light. Keep it simple.

Step Five: Prepare for growth.

In time, those in a group may remember or even discover other gals who might be interested in joining this type of savvy singles society. While inviting close friends or buddies into the circle might seem a good idea, be careful. The point of the club is not to keep your closest friends closer, but to slowly widen your circle, grow your own perspective, and help build up others as well as yourself!

As you look to expand your group, keep in mind that some personalities and backgrounds are like oil and water. Others blend nicely. That's just a fact of life. Being sensitive to the existing group and thoughtful when choosing whom to invite and when to invite them will be worth the effort.

Once your group includes five ladies and looks like it needs to expand, you might consider the group's traveling radius: who travels the farthest when you meet? Often that person—assuming, of course, that she's willing—is a good or natural choice to branch out and start a group closer to where she lives or works. Maybe another person in your group would be willing to help her start that new club over in their neck of the woods. You never know, and you might even be surprised.

When we girls suddenly need to talk, we have a tendency to take the first willing ear offered. That decision may not always be the best decision. A Chix Chat Club can provide a safe place to vent and to seek counsel. Connecting, sharing, and lending a hand is what we solo sisters often need. It's just a matter of getting organized, committing, and making it happen.

I look forward to hearing about your stories of success!

Chix Chat:

1. What thoughts would you share or topics would you discuss with a Chix Chat Club?
2. If your lifestyle or schedule is not conducive to getting together with other girls regularly, what alternative options for staying connected and encouraging like-minded women would you create or suggest? Video conferencing? Skype?
3. How might you convince the right mix of girls of the importance of meeting together on a regular basis?
4. List ideas for helping to make the club and its membership fun and inviting.

CHAPTER 21

Random Confessions of Single Females

"Wit is the salt of conversation, not the food."
—William Hazlitt

As girlfriends grow closer and get to know one another's quirks, we naturally gab about the real issues. In the early days of meeting with your Chix Chat Club, however, you might want to arrive a bit prepared. Showing up with a few icebreakers, or conversation starters, is always a good idea to ensuring time spent together begins and continues in the right direction. Making a list of hot topics relevant to single women is one of the best ways to do this for your savvy singles, get-togethers.

I'm reminded of a magazine called "HER," which includes a very clever section of girls' random confessions. The submissions are anonymous and incredibly telling. Naturally, the exercise got me to thinking: what are we single gals really thinking? And if we were given a chance to be heard, what would we honestly admit to or say? Curious, I sent out an e-mail to all of the single ladies in my address book and offered them the opportunity to sound off on any and every topic.

The following are some of the opinions and pithy responses I received:

Fears/Frustrations

- *I hate that I'm becoming my mother!*
- *I have singleness. It's not a disease. Don't worry, you can't catch it.*

- *I want to trust a man with all my heart, mind, and strength … and am scared to death to do so.*
- *Next time, I am going to hire a guy to take my car into the mechanic.*
- *What bothers me most is what bothers any aging female—getting a mustache, flab, etc. I need more estrogen!*

Sex

- *My friends get married so that they can have sex. Then, come to find out, they don't have it very often.*
- *The trumpet better not sound on the night of my honeymoon!*
- *I miss human touch. I want someone to hold my hand and hug me.*
- *As I get older, I realize that friends don't talk about boyfriends or sex so much. Now we talk about health, aging parents, and their children and grandchildren, and my nieces and nephews, and the moral decay of the nation.*
- *During a recent exam at the gynecologist, my doctor actually asked, "Honey, have you not used this thing in a while?"*

Dating

- *It makes me feel good when gorgeous blondes are just as single as I am.*
- *It irks me that guys my age want to date girls that could be my kid!*
- *Muscular (or cut) men do not need to wear tight t-shirts and jeans at hurch. I am too distracted by them.*
- *I'm not afraid to ask a guy to dance. If I wanna dance, I wanna dance.*
- *I hate when the guy I am dating has no regard for my schedule, as if I am supposed to wait for him to let me know what I am going to do with my nights or weekends!*
- *I hate when the girl who one day is whining about not having a boyfriend suddenly acts like she has all the answers about men once she starts dating one.*
- *What happened to chivalry?*
- *If a single man mentions that he loves sports and I mention that I love sports and would love to catch a game, that is my way of saying, "Ask me out." I hate it when he talks stats instead.*

- *I not only have a list of qualities (I want in a man) written out; I have them posted on the internet on dating sites.*
- *It's frustrating and a shame when a married man will flirt before a single man will.*
- *I'd rather date guys younger than me. Any day!*
- *I love the thrill of still getting butterflies in my stomach when a new guy calls. Would that stop if I was married? I'm afraid it has for some of my married girlfriends.*
- *There's something that feels good about turning the head of a twenty-five-year-old man.*
- *I like older men.*
- *I feel it's okay to remind God that He wrote Ecclesiastes 4:11: "If two lie down together they keep warm, but how can one be warm alone?"*

Singleness and God

- *On healthy days, I believe that God allowed me to be single for a reason. On unhealthy days, I wonder what in the world He's thinking!*
- *I was told to be the right woman and the right man will come along. I feel lied to.*
- *How does the woman who shows no respect to (and gives no time to) her children or her man, get married? Why did God let them become wives and mothers and not me?*

Independence

- *I'm not single because I'm "too independent." I'm a never-married forty-one-year old. This much independence wasn't in my plan.*
- *Just because I have some independence doesn't mean that I want to stay independent and single. I've learned to be independent, make a lot of decisions by myself, and take care of myself simply I had no choice. It's called survival—not independence.*
- *I struggle to know when to ask for help around the house or on my car. Who to ask? Who will truly want to help?*
- *I want to be loved and shown affection so badly.*
- *As the song says, "I need a hero!" People tell me that I'm strong, but I'm yearning for a hero of my own.*

About that Married Crowd ...

- *Sometimes insecure married women think that just because I said hello to their husbands, I'm after them. I'm not!*
- *It's frustrating listening to a married woman gripe and put her husband down when he is a great husband who is faithful, attentive to her needs, loving, and ... need I say more?*
- *When people ask why I'm still single, I say "I'd rather be single and happy than married and miserable."*
- *I'm upset with the pressure to get married.*
- *I wish my married friends wouldn't tell me about their romantic get-a-ways with their husbands.*
- *I hate it when married women feel the need to tell me how sexy their husbands are.*
- *I love how people encourage me to be content in my singleness, then go home to their spouses!*
- *Why do my friends bring their children to lunch with us? All I really need is a listening ear. And it doesn't happen when children are present.*

On The Job

- *Single people should be able to take as many hours and days off for "various reasons" as married people do for "caring for a sick child," "parent/teacher conferences," and "recitals."*
- *If I was married, I would be treated very differently at work.*
- *Sometimes I wish I could call into work and say, "I have singleness. I'm taking the day off. I don't know how long it will last. It may take a little while to recover."*
- *It's unfortunate when work feels its okay to ask the singles to pick up the slack if a married person has a conflict.*

"I Feel Single When ..."

- *I honestly don't think about being single much except when I am in church, and there it tends to get rubbed in a bit.*
- *I get tired having to make all the decisions.*
- *Who brings the soup and the medicine when I'm sick?*

- *I want someone to do things with.*
- *I don't have someone to spoil me.*
- *Even when it's just me, I cook for twenty people.*

Things That Make Life Better

- *A movie is the best therapy.*
- *Cookie dough. Specifically chocolate chip!*
- *I don't know what I would do without my dog.*
- *I frequently enjoy carb-therapy.*
- *When I get the blues, I go shopping.*
- *I have to purposefully surround myself with other singles who are getting the best out of life and giving life back. If I don't, it's easy for me to get down and discouraged.*
- *I like candle-lit bubble baths.*
- *Dancing cheers me up. I go every week.*
- *I enjoy making decisions just for me.*
- *Not having to get anyone else's approval to spend money is nice.*
- *Sometimes I eat an entire bag of potato chips. In one sitting!*
- *I've discovered all the cupcake places in town.*

These poignant, thought-provoking and even hilarious confessions will help get the ball rolling for some delightful girl time. And if you still run out of things to gab about (which I highly doubt) or find things getting off to a slow start, consider sharing some of the words of random wisdom from a few single guys:

- *Don't bring up the "M" word ("Marriage") at all on the first date.*
- *Don't look for a boyfriend if what you really need is a repairman.*
- *Not everything has to be planned.*
- *I haven't had to ask permission to go and workout since I was a kid. Don't make me start now.*
- *Cabinets are made to be used.*
- *The older I get, the more I enjoy being single.*
- *I appreciate simplicity.*
- *Don't think there's a deeper meaning behind everything men say.*

- *If you want me to look deep into your eyes, don't wear an outfit that shows off "the girls."*
- *Just because a guy doesn't want to go out doesn't mean he's angry.*
- *Don't ever let facts get in the way of your good story. (wink)*
- *Don't ask my opinion unless you really want the truth.*
- *Why are women so clingy?*
- *Why do women ask my opinion and then go the opposite direction?*
- *I don't want to hear about old relationships on a date.*
- *Can we talk about me for a minute?*
- *It puts a guy on the spot when a woman asks, "How do I look?"*
- *Asking deep or sincere questions on a first date isn't a good idea.*
- *Women see a pretty deer: men see antlers on the wall.*

Chix Chat:

List your top ten random confessions regarding singleness. Then consider finding some single guys and see if you can get a list from them.

CHAPTER 22

The Upside of Living Single

"Neither should a ship rely on one small anchor nor should life rest on a single hope."
—*Epictetus*

JUST as I sat down to write this chapter, Judge managed to end the life of an unsuspecting ground hog in the back yard. Fortunately, a neighbor came to my rescue and assisted with the clean up. Before he swaggered off with the trash bag that carried the rodent's remains, he looked my dog straight in the eye and uttered the words, "good dog!" As I watched him leave, I found myself thinking; *thank the good Lord for men!*

The single girls I meet and know, some of whom I have introduced to you throughout this book, are attractive, professional, educated, and well-traveled gals. While they agree that it's sometimes rough not to have someone to care for them when they're sick or to cover the bills when they're short on cash or to help with rodent removal and other unpleasant tasks around the house, they know that we single gals are part of a growing club that does enjoy a few perks—sometimes we just have to step back and take a fresh look at them.

Before wrapping up, I want to briefly address that quintessential "What's so great about being single?" question. Since these days people respond to talking points, I came up with a few I can whip out when the need arises. I figured they'd come in handy the next time a sans spouse friend feels a bit blue.

FIVE SINGLE FREEDOMS

While the positive aspects of the single life may vary depending on who you ask, I think that many would agree that being single comes with a healthy dose of freedom. In fact, as I thought about it, I decided that we single gals experience five liberties our married friends might wish they could claim.

1. Freedom to Roam

I've visited Israel, Morocco, Europe, Australia, and a few more fascinating places along the way. I ate St. Peter's fish beside the Sea of Galilee; rode the back of camels—one of which was pregnant and took off running down the coast of the Mediterranean with me astride—; and, in the rain forest down under, I was attacked by a very unhappy three-foot kangaroo. I scaled a waterfall in Jamaica, swam with the stingrays in the Grand Caymans, and snorkeled with the massive turtles in Cozumel. I sunbathed in Puerto Vallarta and took surfing lessons in Hawaii. And on a trip to communist East Germany, I even helped smuggle out documents and personal items belonging to a family trapped behind the iron curtain before the Berlin wall came down.

> Single comes with a healthy dose of freedom.

I also enjoy the freedom to chase work opportunities. I have appeared on the QVC shopping channel, have recorded two independent solo projects, am a member of the Screen Actors Guild, have done musical theatre and even performed in a real Broadway show that re-opened in Los Angeles. (Talk about off, off, Broadway). I do voice over work, and there's always something new on my plate waiting for my attention. Most of the time, I'm free to go where the work takes me.

Flying and driving from location to location is a privilege of sorts for the solo set. And whether her travel budget is large or small, a single girl—especially one without children—is often more apt and able to travel than a woman tied down to daily family responsibilities. While traveling certainly doesn't cure a pang of loneliness, it can certainly help to dull the sting. I think the ability to roam is a pretty amazing opportunity. Even if it's a quick road trip merely to visit a family member or a friend. Sometimes, it just feels good to get away.

2. Freedom to Spend Quality Time with Family.

One year I took ninety-four-year old Gramps to Las Vegas. As I checked into a hotel on the strip with this elderly man who shared my last name, I found myself saying "grandpa" out loud about ten times. I counted heavily on that and my tame and unassuming wardrobe to convince the hotel staff I was not his escort!

As Gramps and I shuffled—and I honestly mean "shuffled"—our way through the casinos and hotels, we had a ball! We viewed the city from the Stratosphere, ate at the Irish Pub in New York, New York, walked the streets at Paris, drank a lot of coffee, and simply talked and watched and laughed. It was well worth the effort and the trip. After Gramps passed away, I found myself reliving those special memories time and time again.

For years I spent my vacations and my spare time hopping among three states. If I was not making the fifteen hour drive to visit my mother, I was on a plane headed towards Gramps' home. For a long time, my vacation days generally went to my family; and I can honestly say that I've enjoyed most of these opportunities.

We singles can often just "go" when we need or want to—job and schedule permitting, of course. Having time free to spend with the people in our lives who mean the most to us is a priceless gift.

3. Freedom to Help a Friend in Need.

Not long ago, I experienced a challenging week in which a number of things on my to-do list got shoved aside so I could assist some dear friends in need. One of these people struggled with a teenager who was experimenting in witchcraft, cutting herself, and trying to "connect" with a person who had passed away years ago. When the teen's mom went to her knees in prayer over her sweet child and dug into the Bible for some much-needed wisdom and answers, she asked me to help. Thankfully, I was able to encourage her through chats over the phone and internet. We also met face-to-face, and I did my best to help her talk and wade through that frightening time.

During the same week, several more friends desperately needed sisterly support. One had just been laid off, her elderly mother was going in for surgery, and she was dealing with a child who battled an addiction. We spent time talking and hashing it through, and she seemed to feel better for having a caring sounding board. Another friend succumbed to the pressure to hurry up and find a mate; she asked me to help her write her online bio. I drove across town to meet with her, and she was grateful for the camaraderie. Yet another friend was re-entering a career and experiencing painful rejection that hurt her deeply. She too needed to know I was in her corner, and I did everything I could to reinforce her self-image. In another situation, a girlfriend's child had been out partying and fell off of a balcony. The student could have died, but God spared him; he was not, however, spared a police record. His mom just needed a listening ear, and I was happy to oblige.

If I were married, I never could have dropped what I was doing to spend hours on the phone, online, or in person just being there for my friends. While I did work and my schedule was full, I could often jump in the car at all hours when they needed me. I am so thankful that singleness provides me time to invest in the relationships in my life, and I am always happy to do so. After all, when I am in need, these same people are there for me in return. It just goes both ways. As it should.

4. Freedom to Eat Whatever, Whenever.

When I have had a rough day, I truly want to go out to an expensive restaurant for what I refer to as gourmet therapy. Since that isn't always a prudent budgetary decision, I usually default to my favorite Mexican place. The staff at this particular eatery all knows me and seem to accept me as extended family. I lovingly refer to this place as my second kitchen; and if I had my way, I would eat there every day.

Sometimes I am forced to go another step down the nutrition ladder and fight off the Krispy Kreme™ attack. (Did I mention I love to eat?) And if I can't afford either the Mexican restaurant or a doughnut, I go home and whip up a batch of chocolate chip cookie dough. Sometimes I bake it.

There's a reason for the expression "comfort food." Eating and food seem connected to our inner beings. I fully realize that we need to watch our calories and everything should be done in moderation, but this girl needs some culinary counseling now and then! Why is food such a comforter? I don't really know, but sometimes I think eating ice cream for breakfast and cookies for dinner could go a long way to melting away the stress.

One of the major perks of singleness—and obviously I'm referring to those of us who don't have kids here—is that our schedules are pretty much our own when it come to when, where, and what we eat. If we can find someone able and willing to grab some Thai cuisine, that's great. And too, we don't have to prepare a separate dish for little "Johnny" if we're cooking, or wonder if someone else may have made other plans for our days, evenings, or weekends that they might have forgotten to tell us about. To some degree, we own our worlds.

5. Freedom to Enjoy Leisure Time—Leisurely.

One morning as the sun shone through the window of my room, I lay in bed just soaking up a morning where I didn't have to rush off to work. My wonderfully patient dog, realizing this change in routine, did not break the silence and allowed my tired bones time to adjust to the reality that lay ahead. Daytime.

When my cell phone rang and interrupted the serenity, I threw back the covers and managed to catch the call before it rolled into voicemail. Chloe's name popped up on the screen, and I began to laugh. It was 8:30 in the morning.

"What?" I answered the phone with a chuckle.

"Let's go to Waffle House!" she said, "I am in the middle of a chick-lit novel, and they are at Waffle House. It's all I can think about. I am going in sweats and have no makeup on. I will pick you up in five minutes."

Fortunately, I had time to feed the dog, change, and brush my teeth before she pulled into the driveway. Then off we went.

Chloe and I both realized that a married woman, or a mother—whether a wife or single—would not have the luxury of this type of last minute decision. We were very aware that we were living a really good life at that moment, and we were grateful. It was a gorgeous fall day, and as we rolled down the road into the morning sun, I read aloud the Waffle House scene from her paperback. It was one of those perfect girl times.

Singleness has moments like this that you and I need and have a right to cherish. But we must remember that we make such experiences happen. I could have very easily ignored Chloe's call or even cancelled on my friend. The excuses I might use are endless: I am depressed, call me later. I have little money. I can't; I'm on a diet. The guy I like blew me off. Work was awful this week, and I need time to re-energize. I have too much to do. This is my only day to get things done. I have to clean … On and on I could have gone, but I didn't. Instead, I seized the moment. And we had a wonderful time!

Singles don't have to juggle a child's soccer game, an office event a spouse needs us to attend, and the pressure of keeping our houses immaculate lest a mother-in-law drops in unannounced. Because of these freedoms, we are often able to be there for people when others are not; we can indulge in some things married girls can't always enjoy; and we can enjoy the luxury of spontaneity.

We can thrive, and not just survive, as singles. But to do so, you and I must seize the day: carpe diem. So, make the most of every opportunity. And as a friend once wisely advised, "When the moment comes, you'll know it. And you'll know how to handle it. Take it. Do it."

Embrace life!

Chix Chat:

1. Describe the most exotic or bizarre place you have visited or seen.
2. Describe an exotic or bizarre place that you would *like* to visit.
3. When was the last time you treated a friend to coffee or lunch?
4. When was the last time you met someone else's need? Explain.
5. Which family member would you take on a special trip or treat to a get-a-way? Why? Where would you go?
6. Describe the craziest, last-minute thing you did with a friend. If you can't think of one, it's past time to get spontaneous. Carpe Diem!

Until We Meet Again ...

> *"Laugh and the world laughs with you.*
> *Cry, and they will look for the nearest exit."*
> — Me

After all the emotional territory we've traversed together in the previous pages, you've likely caught a glimpse—if even a small one—that we single girls just might be a little more blessed than cursed. The upsides of singleness can be simply priceless. And very precious. At least, that's the way I choose to see them.

The Good Lord could let all girls marry early and well in life. He could choose to prevent all husbands from passing away before their brides. And He could hold even the most miserable marriages together. But He doesn't. Rather than bemoaning the facts, we must remember that He gave the gift of life and the ability to experience it to the fullest, allowing us to thrive in our current freedoms.

Sure, at times we single gals will cry out like a friend who confided, "I am just worn out. I recently told God, 'If you aren't bringing someone to me, just take me home, now!'" But those times won't encompass ninety percent of our life and days. They will be only temporary bumps in the road where we hit ice, lose our traction, and spin around a bit. Everyone faces winter seasons—those times that bring a whole set of elements that we can view as cold and dark and overwhelming. But while singleness brings its share of winter, we must look forward to the moments more like spring.

Even when the winter moments come, we can choose to see them as opportunities for a quiet blanket of snow or a fabulous ski trip. I'm reminded of the family ski outing I mentioned earlier. As my teenage cousin, peered at the downhill run that lay before us, I teasingly reminded him, "Jordan. Moguls are our friends." What I really wanted him to hear me say was that, life, like moguls, isn't easy. But methodically facing and embracing it can bring about some very cool adventures and long lasting memories. (Not unlike skiing those moguls!)

Deciding to thrive in the midst of singleness is like coming out of the winter blues and embracing the warmth and beauty of the spring. As I write these closing thoughts, the birds are singing, the sun is trying to break through the clouds, and the buds on the trees are ready to burst forth with all their might. The season past is melting in preparation for something new and fresh around the corner.

If you're in the midst of winter, my friend, please know that spring does come. It's out there. Really. And you and I can help usher in the newness when the time comes—if we so choose.

As we learn to see beauty in the winter moment—like ice on the bare branches outside my window that are so beautiful for a time, we can also come to grips with and embrace that "just around the corner" promise. We can remember that, at any second, things can get drastically better, just as I know that soon the colors will pop out and adorn my landscape and a warm breeze will dance through the flowers.

> Embrace that "just around the corner" promise!

Winter good. Spring better. Enjoy both. And no matter where you may find yourself, let's raise our teacups to laughter, to fun, to like-minded sisters, and to fabulous future road trips with our pets, families, or friends.

So, the next time you see an SUV zooming down the freeway with a black, furry head hanging out the back window, please be sure and wave. It's likely me, probably heading to the nearest Mexican restaurant or coffee house. Come join me, won't you?

Happy Trails and Heart-Felt Hugs,

Stephanie

www.Facebook.com (search for: "Stephanie's Book")
www.Twitter.com/StephaniesBook

Acknowledgments

WHEN I decided to get serious about putting this book on paper, I met with Martha Bolton, script-writer for Bob Hope and author extraordinaire. She had no idea how nervous and tongue-tied I truly was as we lunched together that fall day. I was humbled and more than honored that she'd squeeze me into her schedule. The best advice I received from her? "Put your thoughts into files. Those files become chapters. Keep it funny." With that, I was off and running.

Thank you, Martha!

Gratitude also belongs to the charter members of the first Chix Chat Club: Christa, Janell, Maureen, and Michele. You were my muses for this project, and I thank you from the bottom of my heart. After one particular coffee night we spent together; I went home and wrote in my laptop until 2:00 a.m.! That's when it all truly began.

Amanda, Gina, Gloria, Heather, Kayla, Kim, Koreen, Lauralin, Mary Chris, Melissa L., Melissa W., Nancy, Sharon, Stacey and Tiffany: thank you for your ideas, your stories, and for reading loads of content. Repeatedly. I appreciate your patience and your kindness in commenting and encouraging. I am amazed we got through this and I can still call each of you "friend!"

To the folks at The Journey. Your input, your support, and your comments proved priceless.

Thank you, Jen: What an icon! But our chats and giggles are what I care about most. Thank you for writing my foreword.

Mo—my fab illustrator—may others come to utilize your wonderful talents. I couldn't be happier with what you brought to this book.

Gloria, you have your work cut out for you! Thanks so much for taking me on.

Linden, thank you for helping me find an editor who had no fear and a very large heart. (And an incredible amount of tact.)

Bethany: You taught me to figure out what it was I was actually trying to say, then, simply "say it." Not an easy feat. Thank you for the two-month tutoring session. I think they call it editing. You take spaghetti on paper and somehow help create a work of art. I am blessed to have found you.

And to my mother who endured the toughest weeks with me. In the days when everything about the book process came to a close and I was nothing but raw nerves and anxiety, you read every chapter numerous times. You endured that season with such grace. Thank you, Mom, for all of those lunches and prayers.

And to my grandmother. My rock. Our family's prayer warrior. Grandma, you are truly my "single" hero.

And to Judge. The best dog a single gal could have. Though you'll never read this book, you quietly snoozed through every click of the keys. You will not only live on in my heart, but in these pages for years to come.

Source Notes

Chapter 2

1. Jorge M. Rivas. "Census Bureau: Singles are Increasing Their Influence in America" [online] 18 July 2007 [cited June 6, 2009]. Available from the Internet: *http://www.associatedcontent.com/article/318338/census_ bureau_singles_are_increasing.html?cat=7.*
2. U.S. Census Bureau Newsroom. "Facts for Features: Single Life" [online] 21 July 2008 cited June 4, 2009]. Available from the Internet: *http://www.census.gov/Press-Release/www/releases/archives/facts_for_ features_special_editions/012246.html.*
3. Ibid.
4. Ibid.
5. Ibid.
6. Ibid.
7. Sharon Jayson and Anthony DeBarros. "Young Adults Delaying Marriage" [online] 12 September 2007 [cited 4 June 2009]. Available from the Internet: *http://www.lavoice.org/index.php?name=News&file=ar ticle&sid=2908.*
8. Ibid.
9. Ibid.
10. Jean Twenge. *Generation Me: Why Today's Young Americans Are More Confident, Assertive, Entitled—and More Miserable Than Ever Before* (Free Press, 2007).
11. Unmarried Women — Alarming Statistics" [online] 25 October 2004 [cited 25 July 2009]. Available from the Internet: *http://www.arabnews. com/?page=9&section=0&article=53363&d=25&m=10&y=2004*
12. Unmarried Women Are More Generous Than Unmarried Men" [online] 10 March 2008 [cited 6 June 2009].

Available from the Internet: *http://www.afpnet.org/ka/ka-3.cfm?content_item_id=24400&folder_id=2345*.

13. Ibid.

Chapter 3

1. Bureau of Labor Statistics, U.S. Department of Labor *Occupational Outlook Handbook 2008-2009 Edition*. "Actors, Producers, and Directors" [online] [cited 6 June 2009]. Available from the Internet: *http://www.bls.gov/oco/ocos093.htm*.

Chapter 7

1. "If you want a friend in Washington, get a dog." *Harry S. Truman quotes*, [online] [cited 25 July 2009]. Available from the Internet: *http://en.thinkexist.com/search/searchQuotation.asp?search=%22if+you+want+a+friend+in+Washington%2C+get+a+dog%22*

Chapter 17

1. Katherine Hepburn. *Me: Stories of My Life* (Ballantine Books, 1997). Other biographical information available from the internet. *http://wikipedia.org*. [cited 10 July 2009].

Chapter 19

1. Rosetta Foundation. "Sex for Him/Her" [online] 2009. [cited 15 July 2009]. Available from the Internet: *http://www.teenbreaks.com/hookingup/sexhimher.cfm*.
2. Ibid.
3. Ibid.

For Further Reading

Abortion

O'Neill, Jennifer, *You're Not Alone: Healing Through God's Grace After Abortion*, Deerfield Beach, Faith Communications (HCI Books).

Abstinence

Celebrities who promote Abstinence
http://www.teenbreaks.com/hookingup/celebrityvirgins.cfm.
Secondary Virgins
http://www.teenbreaks.com/hookingup/sexyesno.cfm.
http://Www.TeenBreaks.com Maine, USA, 2009 Rosetta Foundation.

Cancer and The Single Girl

Wolfinger, Cheryl, *6' Tall and Bald*, Raleigh, Lulu.com (Lulu Enterprises, Inc.).

Career Coaching

Miller, Dan, *48 Days to the Work You Love*, Nashville, B&H Publishing Group.

Dating and The Single Girl

Fein, Ellen and Schneider, Sherry, *The Rules*, New York, Warner Books, Inc.
Gray, John, *Mars & Venus on a Date*, New York, Perrenial Currents.
Harvey, Steve, *Act Like a Lady, Think Like a Man: What Men Really Think*

About Love, Relationships, Intimacy, and Commitment, New York, Amistad.

Divorce

O'Neill, Jennifer, *From Fallen To Forgiven*, Nashville, Thomas Nelson.
O'Neill, Jennifer, *Surviving Myself*, New York, William Morrow.

Fiction

O'Neill, Jennifer, *A Fall Together: Circle of Friends-Just off Main*, Nashville, B&H Publishing Group.
O'Neill, Jennifer, *A Late Spring Frost Circle of Friends-Just off Main*, Nashville, B&H Publishing Group.
O'Neill, Jennifer, *A Winter of Wonders Circle of Friends-Just off Main* Nashville, B&H Publishing Group.
(Also available at: *http://www.jenniferoneill.com*).

Financial Coaching

Ramsey, Dave, *The Total Money Makeover: A Proven Plan for Financial Fitness*, Nashville, Thomas Nelson.

Pornography (help with addictions)

http://www.girlsagainstporn.com Los Angeles, CA, 2009.

Sex and The Single Girl

Carrie L. Lukas, *Politically Incorrect Guide to Women, Sex, and Feminism*, Washington, D.C., Regency Publishing.
O'Neill, Jennifer, *Surviving Myself*, New York, William Morrow.

About the Author

STEPHANIE Huffman is a Southern California native who began singing with a seventeen-piece stage band at the age of sixteen. Having a passion for Musical Theatre, Stephanie studied professionally at the Dorothy Chandler Pavilion and Dupree' Dance Academy in Los Angeles. She received her Bachelor of Music degree from the University of Redlands. Stephanie has recorded two independent inspirational music projects and has performed in venues that have led her from San Diego to Spain.

An award-winning stage actress and voice over professional, Stephanie Huffman is also a member of the Screen Actors Guild who has appeared in film, radio, and television. Her credits include projects featuring the likes of LeAnn Rimes, Josh McDowell and more.

In addition to appearances as the on-air spokesperson for B&H Publishing Group on the QVC Shopping Channel, Stephanie has been heard as the Voice of LifeWay Christian Resources and their chain of retail stores.

Stephanie has a passion for teaching the Word of God, and has led teens, collegians, women's and other adult Bible studies for more than two decades. She has also served as the Southeast Director for Women in Christian Media, led its Nashville Connection for two years, and is a board member of Jennifer O'Neill Ministries.

Read more about Stephanie on her website:
http://www.StephanieHuffman.org.

www.ingramcontent.com/pod-product-compliance
Lightning Source LLC
Chambersburg PA
CBHW031551300426
44111CB00006BA/269